Do More Faster

TECHSTARS LESSONS TO ACCELERATE YOUR STARTUP

David Cohen and Brad Feld

WILEY

John Wiley & Sons, Inc.

Published by John Wiley & Sons, Inc., Hoboken, New Jersey.
Published simultaneously in Canada.

For general information on our other products and services or for technical support, please contact our Customer Care Department within the United States at (800) 762–2974, outside the United States at (317) 572–3993 or fax (317) 572–4002.

Wiley also publishes its books in a variety of electronic formats. Some content that appears in print may not be available in electronic books. For more information about Wiley products, visit our web site at www.wiley.com.

Library of Congress Cataloging-in-Publication Data:

Cohen, David G.
  Do more faster : techStars lessons to accelerate your startup / David Cohen and Brad Feld.
       p. cm.
  Includes index.
  ISBN 978-0-470-92983-4 (cloth); ISBN 978-0-470-94877-4 (ebk);
  ISBN 978-0-470-94878-1 (ebk); ISBN 978-0-470-94879-8 (ebk)
  1. New business enterprises–Management.   2. Entrepreneurship.
I. Feld, Brad.   II. Title.
  HD62.5.C635 2011
  658.1′1–dc22

                                                    2010033309

Printed in the United States of America.

10 9 8 7 6 5 4 3 2 1

To our wives—Amy Batchelor and Jil Cohen—with
happy amazement that they love us.

Contents

Foreword

While entrepreneurs come in all shapes and sizes, they all share the drive to do things that have never been done before, the belief that they can accomplish anything they put their minds to, and the need to get everything done as fast as they can. For a first time entrepreneur, this can be daunting, but TechStars is like a turbo rocket booster for the beginning of the journey.

Zynga is my fourth company. When I started it, there were only a few venture capitalists who I wanted to work with, and Brad Feld was one of them. The last few years have been a wild ride. We talk about doing things at "Zynga Speed" so when Brad asked me to write a foreword for a book titled *Do More Faster*, I was humbled and eager to have the opportunity to share some thoughts, as this is a concept that is close to my heart.

If you aren't familiar with Zynga, we are the makers of popular social games such as FarmVille, FrontierVille, and Mafia Wars. When Brad's firm Foundry Group invested in Zynga in the fall of 2007, we were a team of 10 people. Today, three years later, we are a family of more than 1,200 people. To get there, we certainly had to do more faster.

Before starting my first company in the mid-1990s, I worked at several well-regarded companies. However, I was somewhat of a misfit. I challenged the status quo and didn't necessarily follow protocol. I was a bit naïve and rogue in my desire to deliver the smartest and most strategic results without being concerned with procedures. That wasn't necessarily the best way to ensure a career in corporate America, so I decided I was better suited to be an entrepreneur where I could do things my way.

At the dawn of the commercial Internet, I co-founded Freeloader with Sunil Paul. As first-time entrepreneurs, we learned as we went along and made plenty of mistakes along the way. What we lacked in experience, we made up for in drive, and before we knew it, we were at the helm of a hot new Internet company funded by Flatiron Partners and SOFTBANK. Four months after our first round of financing, Freeloader was acquired by Individual, Inc. for $38 million. While this was viewed as a success, the acquisition happened well before the moment of truth for our business.

When I founded my second company, SupportSoft, I had a bit more experience and made building a great startup team a priority. We accomplished exciting things together and built the company into a leading provider for service and support automation software. As the company began to achieve customer and revenue traction and acceleration, I agreed to move into the position of chairman as the board wanted to bring in a more seasoned CEO. SupportSoft was successful, went public, and everyone was happy, but I still didn't feel like I'd had a chance to build a great company.

My third company was Tribe Networks. The idea of social networks was starting to emerge and Tribe was one of the very first. I like to say that Tribe was a great idea, just ahead of its time. We had early success, raised money from venture capitalists, but over time we stumbled. I was once again promoted to chairman and this time the new leadership failed to execute. Near the end, I stepped back in as CEO and repositioned the company around white label hosting of social media. We sold the company for a modest amount to Cisco, but we missed a huge opportunity to create a next-generation Internet company.

So, in 2007 when I started thinking about social gaming, I decided that my goal with Zynga was to create a company that consumers would know and love. I wanted to create an Internet treasure. Unlike at my previous companies, I focused my early recruiting efforts on attracting investors who would act as peers, respect what I wanted to accomplish, and help coach me through the ups and downs of the business. In addition to Brad, I was fortunate to attract Fred Wilson, Bing Gordon, and Reid Hoffman as investors and board members to Zynga early on. We've accomplished a lot in the past three years and I believe we are well on our way to creating a company that will stand the test of time and have a lasting impact on consumers and the Internet as a whole.

When I reflect on my entrepreneurial experiences over the past 15 years, I recognize the critical importance of learning from mistakes. Every company had roadblocks and challenges, and at each step and with each setback, I became smarter. It took a long time and a lot of ups and downs to get to the point where I was ready to embark on the creation of Zynga. I wish I'd had more of that knowledge and insight when I started FreeLoader, or had access to the wisdom and experiences like those shared in this book.

The entrepreneurial journey is an amazing one that I encourage anyone who has the inclination to embark on. There are few things as rewarding as starting a business from nothing, creating jobs, and building something that matters. There is something unique that ties all entrepreneurs together, and we have a strong desire to see one another succeed and a belief in the importance of entrepreneurship. I am encouraged to see the support and tools that first-time entrepreneurs today have such as TechStars, books like *Do More Faster*, and the support of many great experienced entrepreneurs including those in this book. I am honored to be one of those mentors and am excited to see what the next wave of entrepreneurs create. They will learn, just as I did, that they can always Do More Faster!

Mark Pincus
August 2010

Preface

Entrepreneurship is hard. Most startup companies fail. Even those entrepreneurs who have achieved success often have stories of staggering personal challenges and failures. The bone yard of unsuccessful entrepreneurial endeavors is very wide and very deep.

Enter TechStars, a mentorship-driven seed accelerator that has helped numerous fledgling companies attract over $25 million in venture capital and angel investment. How have so many founders of TechStars companies already gone on to sell their companies and to make millions so quickly? Why has TechStars generated so many disruptive and innovative companies?

It's the mentorship.

Having worked with thousands of entrepreneurs and hundreds of companies over the past 25 years, we have seen a number of issues come up over and over again. TechStars was created as a way to channel that experience for the benefit of first time entrepreneurs. But we didn't do it alone—we recruited more than 100 of the best Internet entrepreneurs on the planet to become mentors in the program.

Do More Faster was written to capture the TechStars mentors' unique insights into what it takes to make a startup successful. We thought hard about the key issues around early-stage entrepreneurship and organized them around seven themes: Idea and Vision, People, Working Effectively, Product, Fundraising, Legal and Structure, and Work and Life Balance.

Each theme or part contains a number of chapters that focus on common sayings heard around TechStars. Some of these sayings, such as the title of this book, are mantras of ours. A few are well-worn clichés. All of them are critical ideas that can help you be successful as an entrepreneur.

While mastering these themes doesn't ensure success for every first-time entrepreneur, our experience is that understanding the challenges and hearing personal stories and advice from mentors is a large part of it. If nothing else, you'll realize that you aren't alone in facing these challenges.

We asked many of the mentors and entrepreneurs in the program to write chapters and we wrote a few ourselves. TechStars is a magical thing, but it's also very personal and many of the lessons in this book are based upon personal experience. For that reason, we have included as many photos as we could to bring the stories to life. The stories form a cohesive narrative, but they're also strong on their own.

In the spirit of TechStars, this book is community-oriented and mentorship-driven. We hope you'll find the perspectives and stories in this book to be powerful and useful. Let us know what you think. You can reach us at david@techstars.org or brad@feld.com. Or come visit us at TechStars.org.

David Cohen and Brad Feld
August 2010
Boulder, Colorado

About TechStars

T echStars is a mentorship-driven startup accelerator with operations in Boulder, Boston, and Seattle. Once a year in each city we bring together about 10 Internet startups with about 50 top Internet entrepreneurs and investors for a three-month intensive program. More than 600 companies apply every year for one of the 10 spots. The program culminates with an event at which the young startups pitch their ideas to hundreds of investors.

Since its founding in 2006, TechStars has funded 41 companies in Boulder, 19 companies in Boston, and 10 companies in Seattle. About 70 percent of these companies have gone on to raise more than $25 million in angel or venture capital, have become profitable, or have been bought by notable companies such as AOL, Jive Software, IAC, and Automattic (the makers of WordPress). The latest class of Boulder companies resulted in six companies being funded by venture capital firms and two others by angel investors.

We believe that TechStars represents something special. We're often told that it feels like an entrepreneurial revival. The reason for this is best understood by focusing on two things: mentorship and community.

You'll often hear us describe TechStars as "mentorship driven." Each mentor who participates is asked to focus on a single company or at most two if he has a great deal of free time. We carefully avoid the sort of fly-by mentorship in which someone successful or famous stops by to impart some generic wisdom and give shallow feedback on each company. At TechStars, we're only interested in deep and engaged mentorship. Our model typically results in four to six mentors working closely in a focused manner with each company over the course of the three-month program. This is the magic of TechStars—several amazing mentors paired with each company pushing them to be the best that they can be.

TechStars is also about community. When we started TechStars, one of our primary goals was to improve our entrepreneurial ecosystem. We wanted more passionate and skilled businesspeople in Boulder, where we both live. We wanted to engage local angel investors and to create more of them. We wanted Boulder to be known to the world as a credible place for talented entrepreneurs. We wanted the best, brightest, and most experienced entrepreneurs to become mentors and work together on new and exciting startups. Fundamentally, we wanted our community to be better. We're often asked why the mentors in the program help as much as they do. We firmly believe that each and every one of them does it for these same reasons.

We believe that a culture of sustained mentorship is the secret weapon of successful entrepreneurial communities. Because of Tech-Stars, we've noticed that mentorship and community have begun to come full circle. The founders of early TechStars companies are now mentors to the founders of newer ones as well as other companies in their communities. Some of the founders who have been through TechStars are starting their second company. They've been shown the life-changing value of highly engaged mentorship and it is now ingrained into the very fabric of who they are. In turn, they give back every day.

THEME 1: IDEA AND VISION

Most people think that the core of a startup is a singular amazing world-changing and earth-shattering idea. It turns out that this idea is almost always completely wrong.

It has often been said that most successful startups started doing something else. In our experience at TechStars, we know that many of the companies that have gone through the program are now working on something very different from their original idea. Some of these are in the same general domain but a completely different application or product area. A surprising number of them are unrecognizable from the description of their business on the original application to TechStars.

When Alex White of Next Big Sound showed up at TechStars he was immediately confronted by a chorus of "We love you but your idea sucks." Jeff Powers and Vikas Reddy spent the summer working on some sort of image compositing software before landing on the spectacularly successful RedLaser iPhone app that eBay recently acquired. We aren't even sure we remember what Joe Aigboboh and Jesse Tevelow of J-Squared Media were working on when they showed up at TechStars but we had a feeling they were awesome, which they then demonstrated by launching a series of successful Facebook applications on the heels of Facebook's F8 launch. Each of them landed in very interesting but unpredictable places.

Startups are about testing theories and quickly pivoting based on feedback and data. Only through hundreds of small—and sometimes large—adjustments does the seemingly overnight success emerge.

Trust Me, Your Idea Is Worthless

Tim Ferriss

Tim is the best-selling author of The 4-Hour Workweek *(New York: Random House, 2007) as well as an angel investor and an entrepreneur. Tim has been a TechStars mentor since 2008 and is an investor in several TechStars companies, including DailyBurn (the premier fitness social network for detailed tracking, online accountability, and motivation) and Foodzie (an online marketplace where consumers can discover and buy food directly from small artisan producers).*

Photo Courtesy of Corey Arnold

Earth-shattering and world-changing ideas are a dime a dozen. In fact, that's being too generous.

I've had hundreds of would-be entrepreneurs contact me with great news: They have the next big thing, but they can't risk telling me (or anyone else) about it until I sign some form of idea insurance, usually a nondisclosure agreement (NDA). Like every other sensible investor on the planet, I decline the request to sign the NDA, forgoing the idea, often to the shock, awe, and dismay of the stunned entrepreneur.

Why do I avoid this conversation? Because entrepreneurs who behave this way clearly overvalue ideas and therefore, almost by definition, undervalue execution. Brainstorming is a risk-free, carefree activity. Entrepreneurship in the literal sense of "undertaking" is not.

Strap on your seat belt if you're signing up for a startup. It's a high-velocity experience.

If you have a brilliant idea, it's safe to assume that a few very smart people are working on the same thing, or working on a different approach to solving the same problem. Just look at the number of different travel apps on your iPhone or the number of diet and exercise sites on the Web for an example of this.

Overvaluing the idea is a red flag, particularly in the absence of tangible progress. Sure, I miss out on investing in some truly great ideas with this attitude, but that's okay with me: I don't invest in ideas. Nor does Warren Buffett. I'll lose less money than those who do. I can largely control my downside by investing in good people who, even if they fail this go-round, will learn from mistakes and have other fundable ideas (ideas I'll likely have access to as an early supporter). I do not have this advantage when investing in ideas.

One popular startup dictum worth remembering is "One can steal ideas, but no one can steal execution or passion." Put in another light: there is no market for ideas. Think about it for a second: have you tried selling an idea lately? Where would you go to sell it? Who would buy it? When there is no market, it is usually a very sure sign that there is no value.*

Almost anyone can (and has!) come up with a great idea, but only a skilled entrepreneur can execute it. *Skilled* in this case doesn't mean experienced; it means flexible and action-oriented, someone who recognizes that mistakes can often be corrected, but time lost postponing a decision is lost forever. Ideas, however necessary, are not sufficient. They are just an entry ticket to play the game.

Don't shelter and protect your startup concept like it's a nest egg. If it's truly your only viable idea, you won't have the creativity to adapt when needed (and it will be needed often) in negotiation or responding to competitors and customers. In this case, it's better to call it quits before you start.

Your idea is probably being worked on by people just as smart as you are.

Focus on where most people balk and delay: exposing it to the real world. If you're cut out for the ride, this is also where all the

---

*Yes, there are a few exceptions, like licensing IP, but IP is "property," as distinct from an unprotectable thought.

rewards and excitement live, right alongside the 800-pound gorillas and cliffside paths. That's the fun of it.

David didn't beat Goliath with a whiteboard. Go get amongst it, and prepare to bob and weave.

What about all those great ideas we fund at TechStars? Well, about 40 percent of the companies who go through TechStars describe themselves as "substantially or completely different" in regard to the idea and product they're building after the three-month program ends. When the founders of Next Big Sound applied to TechStars, they had an idea around music and social networking. We loved the founders but hated the idea. They were already contemplating changing their idea when they arrived in Boulder in the summer of 2009 but were nervous about what our reaction would be. They quickly heard that we believed in them, not their idea, and aggressively changed course. Alex White, the CEO of Next Big Sound, talks more about this in the chapter "Fail Fast." The willingness to change your idea based on data is the sign of a strong entrepreneur, not a weak one.

Tim Ferriss (second from left) hanging out at the St. Julien hotel in Boulder with Vanilla, Next Big Sound, and Graphic.ly during the summer of 2009.

Start With Your Passion

Kevin Mann

Kevin is the founder and CTO of Graphic.ly, a social digital distribution platform for comic book publishers and fans. Graphic.ly raised $1.2 million from DFJ Mercury, Starz Media, Chris Sacca, and others after completing TechStars in 2009. Kevin also recruited Micah Baldwin, a TechStars mentor, to join Graphic.ly as CEO in the fall of 2009.

I am a huge comic book fan and I started my company because of my own frustration and disappointment.

A few years ago, I read about the release of a new "Dead@17" story and I was excited to find that for once my local comics bookstore actually had it. I bought the first three issues and loved them. I couldn't wait to pick up the fourth and final one.

On the day of the release of that fourth issue, I ran to the comics bookstore. I looked at the new release shelf only to find that it wasn't there. I asked the store owner about it. I was told that because of budget cuts he had to stop buying a bunch of titles and this was one of them. However, he said his sister store in Newcastle had it.

Newcastle was a 100-mile round trip and at the time I didn't drive, so I knew the journey was going to suck. I headed off to the train station and I took my iPod along to make the journey bearable. A couple of hours later I arrived at the Newcastle comic store only to discover that the fourth issue of Dead@17 was sold out there!

On the train on the way home, my frustration and anger boiled over. I kept thinking that there had to be a better way of buying comics. And then it dawned on me. That morning I had purchased a movie from iTunes, which I was watching right there on the train. Why shouldn't buying comics be just as easy? Why did I have to travel over a 100 miles and waste the better part of a day, all for nothing?

I realized that I had two options. I could quit buying comics or I could quit my job and build the iTunes of comics.

That's how Graphic.ly started and my enthusiasm for comics has now transferred to a business I love being a part of. Every single day I am excited to go to work. I get to create and innovate in a sector I love. Ultimately, I'll solve a problem that was ruining something very special to me.

If you're not passionate about what you're doing, it won't mean enough to you to succeed. Startup founders choose an insanely difficult path, so passion is a prerequisite.

Many entrepreneurs start a company to "scratch their own itch." Kevin is a great example of one such entrepreneur as you just read in the story of how he came up with the idea for Graphic.ly. Kevin and his business partner, Than, got right down to building a demo during the TechStars program. They quickly produced a beautiful piece of software for rendering comic books on the web and on an iPhone. One of their mentors, Micah Baldwin, fell in love with the idea and Kevin recruited Micah to join the team as CEO at the end of the summer. Micah, Kevin, and Than quickly raised a seed round of investment from VCs and angels and began building out the team and the product.

One of Graphic.ly's goals was to produce comics with amazing graphic clarity regardless of the platform the comic book was rendered on. They also wanted to innovate in the user interface to add a social component to the comic book, allowing fans to interact with the comics in a deep and engaged way. At the same time, they started building out a library of comics with several of the larger comic book publishers. While there is always a chance that existing e-book vendors will start focusing on comic books, Graphic.ly believes that their single-minded focus on comics gives them a big advantage over other companies.

Kevin also shares the honor of being one of the TechStars Boulder 2009 founders who inspired Brad to co-found the Startup Visa initiative (see startupvisa.com). The goal of the Startup Visa initiative is to make it easy for non-U.S. entrepreneurs to get a visa to start a company in the United States. It turns out to be surprisingly difficult to do this, as Kevin (a U.K. citizen) and Than (a French citizen) discovered. As of July 2010, there are now bills in the U.S. House of Representatives (sponsored by Jared Polis (D-CO) and a co-founder of TechStars) and in the U.S. Senate (co-sponsored by John Kerry (D-MA), Richard Lugar (R-IN), and Mark Udall (D-CO)) and the Startup Visa initiative has continued to build momentum as a grassroots effort.

Look for the Pain

Isaac Saldana

Isaac is the founder and CEO of SendGrid, an e-mail service that solves the problems faced by companies sending application-generated transactional e-mail, which raised $5.75 million from Highway 12, SoftTech VC, and Foundry Group after completing TechStars in 2009.

I have always been interested in solving complicated problems and am naturally passionate about scalability and complex engineering problems. I enjoy using technologies such as Hadoop for massive data analysis, Memcached for distributed caching, and Twisted for event-driven programming. Early in my software engineering career I landed positions as CTO in multiple startups. The more I dealt with engineering problems, the less I wanted to be engaged with users or any other nontechnical problem. I strongly believed that my time was best spent on solving really difficult technical problems instead of dealing with all those pesky customers.

One day I was in the process of moving our static files to Amazon S3 to solve some scalability issues with our web site when one of those annoying users notified us that the e-mails that our application was generating were not getting through to his Yahoo! Mail inbox. Off I went to solve this seemingly trivial problem.

After a few tests I realized that Yahoo! was flagging all of our e-mails as spam. Since this was out of my control, I contacted Yahoo! to solve what I thought would be a trivial nontechnical problem so I could go back to my fun and complicated Amazon S3 project. Yahoo! replied to my request warning me that our company was not following well-known standards to deliver e-mail and that certain content was consistently triggering their spam filter.

I researched this and looked for solutions. But the available solutions were not straightforward. Ultimately, I spent weeks understanding the issues, fine tuning our servers, altering our code, and working with ISPs. I kept thinking about how lucky my company was that I was an experienced and motivated software developer with extensive systems administration experience. Most of the people who were being affected by the problem didn't even know it!

One weekend I thought about how ironic it was that a solution to one problem (spam filtering technology) had introduced another critical problem. Spam filters were filtering out most of the spam e-mails but legitimate e-mails were also being filtered! I wondered how many other subtle problems relating to e-mail existed, and to my surprise, there were many. I started wondering if I had e-mail deliverability issues with other ISPs. What happened to e-mails after they were delivered? Who was opening and clicking on links in my e-mails? Why did companies with applications that generated legitimate transactional e-mail have to worry about CAN-SPAM laws in the first place? It occurred to me that there must be thousands of companies having the kinds of problems that I had just experienced.

Sure enough, I found a report that said that a major electronic commerce vendor loses $14 million dollars for every 1 percent of their legitimate e-mail that is not delivered. So I went deeper.

I started speaking with companies that managed application-generated e-mail. I learned that my theory was correct. Many of them knew that too many of their legitimate e-mails were being trapped by spam filters and almost all of them were simply living with the pain because they didn't know how or have the time to fix it. So I built SendGrid, which makes solving this problem a trivial exercise.

When I offered dozens of companies SendGrid for $100 per month, they all said yes. I raised the price to $300 per month, and they all said yes. $500?—yes. Today, we are working with hundreds of companies, including well-known ones like Foursquare, Gowalla, and GetSatisfaction. When you're selling a solution to a problem and you find that nobody is saying no to your prices, you've found some serious pain. We're building SendGrid to solve a very specific problem that I discovered just by paying attention.

Many TechStars founders—like Isaac—are deeply technical. As you have just read, SendGrid emerged from a specific pain that Isaac encountered in a previous job. While Internet e-mail has been around for a very long time, and commercial Internet e-mail has been around for more than 15 years, new issues continue to arise. Isaac took a fresh look at the problem as a user and realized that even though there are many companies addressing different aspects of e-mail, no one was solving the specific problem he faced.

When we first met Isaac, we knew that he was a technical rock star and had done some clever things, but we didn't realize the breadth and impact of the approach he was taking to solving this problem. Furthermore, nor did he, as it wasn't clear how much people would be willing to pay. We encouraged Isaac to just get out there, talk to, and sign up customers.

Initially, this kind of activity wasn't in Isaac's comfort zone, as he would rather sit in front of his computer and hack on code. But we, and his TechStars mentors, pushed him to go talk to people. At first he talked to other software developers who typically came back with uniformly positive responses. Then he started talking to nontechnical executives of other web companies who were equally enthusiastic. Within a few weeks, Isaac realized how powerful it was to talk to the early users, as they all quickly signed up, started using SendGrid, and gave him immediate feedback on their specific pain, resulting in a much more relevant product.

Billions of e-mails later, it's clear now that SendGrid solves a very real pain.

Get Feedback Early

Nate Abbott and Natty Zola

Nate and Natty are the co-founders of Everlater, an easy and fun way to share your travel experiences. Everlater raised an undisclosed amount from Highway 12 Ventures after completing TechStars in 2009.

When we set out to build a travel web site, we were two finance professionals with zero practical knowledge of software development or how to run an Internet company. We didn't know what we didn't know. So, as an absolute necessity, we set out to share our ideas early and often with as many smart people as we could find.

First, we reached out to any of our friends and family who would talk to us. While our network wasn't rich with savvy Internet personalities or experienced engineers, we knew a lot of folks who wanted to see us succeed—and most of them traveled! We talked to them about how they found hotels, whether they liked scrapbooks, and whom they trusted online. We shared our opinions and received loads of feedback. From this, we stitched together a Frankenstein monster of an idea from our experiences, perceived market needs, and the invaluable advice of friends and family.

With our Franken-idea in hand, we set out to implement it. However, since we were new to programming, we had no experience and few resources with which to teach ourselves. As a result, we turned to the developer community with questions and open minds. Without their support, guidance, and ideas, we would have been lost. It also made our project more fun, as we got lots of smart developers helping us to realize our idea. Many of their suggestions became the backbone of our company.

Finally, we had to turn our science project into a real company. Our philosophy was to meet with anyone and everyone we could. We never knew what experience or ideas would come from the people we met and we believed people have a sneaky way of surprising you with the unexpected.

As we progressed, we realized that even experienced entrepreneurs forget to get enough feedback on their ideas. We regularly experience this every time we use a piece of software or web service that isn't well thought out. Now, even as we become a more mature (although still very young) company, we still share ideas early and often, not just with mentors, but also with our customers and partners. We hope that the advice we're gleaning today will pay dividends as large as the ones we've already received.

Now that we get asked to give feedback to other startups we meet, we see a clear pattern. Many entrepreneurs are hesitant to share too much about what they're doing and, even when they do, they hold back some of their thoughts even when talking to people who could be incredibly helpful to them. These entrepreneurs overvalue their ideas. They should be doing the opposite and shout about what they are working on from any rooftop they can find. Getting feedback and new ideas is the lifeblood of any startup. There is no point in living in fear of someone stealing your idea.

David Cohen once told us that you can steal ideas, but you can't steal execution. As first-time entrepreneurs, we quickly realized that we had many ideas every day—some good ones but many that were crummy. As we discarded the crummy ideas and started focusing on the good ideas, we realized how difficult it was to implement them well. We concentrated—with our small team—on becoming execution machines, as we decided that this was going to be the key to turning our Franken-idea into something amazing.

By sharing our ideas with smart people, the early advice and feedback gave us a wealth of ideas and options to consider and a framework with which to address the important questions that arise while starting a business. It helped us get into TechStars, where we were lucky to build a network of people who understood and were involved with our idea to help solve the problems we faced on a day-to-day basis. As a result, we've found great mentors, made lifelong friends, and enabled ourselves to build a much better business.

Nate and Natty wouldn't have been accepted into TechStars if they hadn't been naturally good at sharing their ideas early and often and seeking feedback. We met them about six months before they applied to TechStars. At first, we were skeptical because they were just two ex–Wall Street guys with no technical skills or experience. We kept in touch with them while they taught themselves how to program and made significant progress on the product in a short time. We were amazed, and encouraged them to apply to TechStars. This was a direct result of Nate and Natty sharing their ideas with us early.

By the way, we are often asked if you have to be technical to start an Internet company. While it certainly helps, Nate and Natty taught us that it's not a requirement. They also taught us that if you aren't technical, there's no reason why you can't learn how to be a software developer if you are a smart human who can learn how to sling code. Their story inspired Brad to write a series called "Learning to Program" on his blog.

Natty and Nate from Everlater, doing more faster during the summer of 2009.

Usage Is Like Oxygen for Ideas

Matt Mullenweg

Matt is the founder of Automattic which makes WordPress.com, Akismet, bbPress, BuddyPress, and now Intense Debate, a TechStars company that Automattic acquired in 2008.

I like Apple because they are not afraid of getting a basic 1.0 out into the world and iterating on it. A case in point:

"No wireless. Less space than a nomad. Lame."—cmdrtaco, Slashdot.org, 2001, when reviewing the first iPod.

I remember my first iPhone. I stood in line for hours to buy it, and like a great meal, you have to wait for in a long line outside a hot night club, the wait made the first time I swiped to unlock the phone that much sweeter. I felt like I was on Star Trek and this was my magical tricorder—a tricorder that constantly dropped calls on AT&T's network, had a headphone adapter that didn't fit any of the hundreds of dollars worth of headphones I owned, ran no applications, had no copy and paste, and was slow as molasses.

Now the crazy thing is when the original iPhone went public, flaws and all, you know that in a secret room somewhere on Apple's campus they had a working prototype of the 3GS with a faster processor, better battery life, and a normal headphone jack—basically everything perfect. Steve Jobs was probably already carrying around one in his pocket. How painful it must have been to have everyone criticizing them for all the flaws they had already fixed but couldn't release yet because they were waiting for component prices to come down or for some bugs to be resolved.

"$400 for an MP3 Player! I'd call it the Cube 2.0 as it won't sell, and be killed off in a short time . . . and it's not really functional. Uuhh, Steve, can I have a PDA now?"—elitemacor, macrumors.com, 2001, responding to the original iPod announcement.

Or, I wonder, is Apple really very zen about the whole thing. There was a dark time in WordPress development history that I call our lost year. Version 2.0 was released on December 31, 2005, and Version 2.1 came out on January 22, 2007. From the dates you might imagine that perhaps we had some sort of rift in the open source community, that all the volunteers left, or that perhaps WordPress just slowed down.

In fact, it was just the opposite—2006 was a breakthrough year for WordPress in many ways. WordPress was downloaded 1.5 million times that year and we started to get some high-profile blogs switching over from other blogging platforms. Our growing prominence had attracted a ton of new developers to the project and we were committing new functionality and fixes faster than we ever had before.

What killed us that year was "one more thing." We could have easily done three major releases that year if we had just drawn a line in the sand and shipped the darn thing. The problem is that the longer it has been since your last release, the more pressure and anticipation there is, so you're more likely to try to slip in just one more thing or a fix that will make a feature really shine. For some projects, this can feel like it goes on forever.

"Hey—here's an idea, Apple—rather than enter the world of gimmicks and toys, why don't you spend a little more time sorting out your pathetically expensive and crap server lineup? Or are you really aiming to become a glorified consumer gimmicks firm?"—Pants, macrumors.com, 2001.

I imagine prior to the launch of the iPod (or the iPhone) there were teams saying the same thing. The copy and paste guys were so close to being ready and they knew Walt Mossberg was going to ding them, so they must have thought "Let's just not ship to the manufacturers in China for just a few more weeks." They were probably pretty embarrassed. But if you're not embarrassed when you ship your first version, you waited too long.

A beautiful thing about Apple is how quickly they make their own products obsolete. I imagine this also makes the discipline of shipping things easier. As I mentioned before, the longer it's been since the last release, the more pressure there is. But if you know that your bit of code doesn't make this version but there's the +0.1 coming out in six weeks, then it's not that bad. It's like flights from San Francisco to Los Angeles; if you miss one, you know there's another one an hour later, so it's not a big deal.

Usage is like oxygen for ideas. You can never fully anticipate how an audience is going to react to something you've created until it's out there. That means every moment you're working on something without it being in the public arena, it's actually dying, deprived of the oxygen of the real world. It's even worse because development doesn't happen in a vacuum. If you have a halfway decent idea, you can be certain that there are at least a few other teams somewhere in the world independently working on the same thing. Something you haven't even imagined could disrupt the market you're working in. Just consider all the podcasting companies that existed before iTunes incorporated podcasting functionality and wiped them all out.

By shipping early and often you have the unique competitive advantage of getting useful feedback on your product. In the best case, this helps you anticipate market direction, and in the worst case, it gives you a few people rooting for you that you can e-mail when your team pivots to a new idea.

You think your business is different, you're going to have only one shot at press, and everything needs to be perfect for when TechCrunch brings the world to your door. But if you have only one shot at getting an audience, you are doing it wrong.

After the debacle of the v2.0 to v2.1 lost year of 2006, the Word-Press community adopted a fairly aggressive schedule of putting a major release out three times a year.

I love working on web services and pretty much everything Automattic focuses on is a service. On WordPress.com, we deploy code to production 20 or 30 times a day and anyone in the company can do it. We measure the deploy time to hundreds of servers and if it gets too slow (more than 30 to 60 seconds), we figure out a new way to optimize it.

In a rapid iteration environment, the most important thing isn't necessarily how perfect code is when you send it out, but how quickly you can revert. This keeps the cost of a mistake really low, under a minute of brokenness. Someone can go from idea to working code to production and, more importantly, real users in just a few minutes, and I can't imagine any better form of testing.

"Real artists ship."—Steve Jobs, 1983

When Brad first met Matt, they had dinner at a nice restaurant in Palo Alto. Matt was too young to drink—and admitted it. As a result, the other person they were dining with (Jeff Clavier, another TechStars mentor) and Brad had to drink all the wine. Brad fell in love with Matt and his vision for WordPress at that dinner and became a huge Matt and WordPress fan. (We are now investors due to Automattic's acquisition of Intense Debate, a TechStars 2007 company.)

Matt's contribution to TechStars can't be understated. In addition to spending time in Boulder each summer and meeting with each TechStars team, Matt serves as a huge inspiration for any first-time entrepreneur who has a vision to create something transformational. And yes, Matt is now old enough to drink.

Matt Mullenweg places the first live order on Foodzie.com at TechStars during the summer of 2008.

Forget the Kitchen Sink

David Cohen

David is the co-founder and CEO of TechStars.

I've seen "everythingitis" kill many a startup. This is the disease a startup gets when it sets out to add more features than the competition does. This is a fundamentally flawed strategy that presumes that users will adopt a new service just because it has more features. The reality is that most people use a particular service because it does one thing really, really well. Think about your own experiences and you'll understand that this is true.

I've been guilty of trying to solve problems by throwing in more and more features, including the kitchen sink. iContact* was the

---

*Note: You might have heard of iContact, but it's not the one that I worked on. The domain name was recycled and today iContact is an e-mail marketing company that is very successful. My friend Ryan Allis runs it. Yes, I sold him the domain name after my iContact failed. It was the most revenue my failed company ever had!

second startup that I founded and it had a serious case of everything-itis. I proudly told everyone that iContact did more than any other mobile social networking product that existed at the time. But the market said: "So what?" No one understood what iContact did better than anybody else in the world, including us. When it didn't take off, we made the fatal mistake of responding by adding more features (including several shiny new kitchen sinks) when we probably should have been removing them and focusing more on the few things that our users did like. iContact eventually died, and that's how I learned this lesson firsthand.

Several TechStars companies came in with a plan like "MySpace + FaceBook + YouTube + kitchen sink." We coached them early on that they have to be the best in the world at something and then build from there. We asked them to focus on their passion and to pick the smallest meaningful problem that they could solve better than anyone in the world had ever done before.

I love what Ev Williams (founder of Odeo, Blogger, Twitter) says about this:

> Focus on the smallest possible problem you could solve that would potentially be useful. Most companies start out trying to do too many things, which makes life difficult and turns you into a me-too. Focusing on a small niche has so many advantages: With much less work, you can be the best at what you do. Small things, like a microscopic world, almost always turn out to be bigger than you think when you zoom in. You can much more easily position and market yourself when more focused. And when it comes to partnering, or being acquired, there's less chance for conflict. This is all so logical and, yet, there's a resistance to focusing. I think it comes from a fear of being trivial. Just remember: If you get to be #1 in your category, but your category is too small, then you can broaden your scope and you can do so with leverage.

Ev's last point is key. If you're the best in the world at thing X, it's much easier to get to X + Y. You'll have credibility from your customers who already love you for what you do so well. They'll be patient and willing to help you build Y. It's a place of strength, and it can be so much easier to do more from there.

If you're early in the life of your startup, do yourself a favor and figure out what one thing you're going to be the best in the world at doing. By all means, don't stop there. Just spend some time to think about how you can cross the finish line and avoid throwing in the kitchen sink. The market will love you for it.

Find That One Thing They Love

Darren Crystal

Darren was the co-founder and CTO of Photobucket, a photo sharing company that was acquired by News Corp in 2007 for about $250 million. He's been a TechStars mentor since 2007.

Shortly before Alex Welch and I co-founded Photobucket in 2003, Alex had launched a photo sharing site in which we noticed that people were doing something that we didn't want them to do. We had intended them to share photos with one another, but they were embedding their photos on other sites on the web.

At first, our natural instinct was to shut this behavior down because it's not what we wanted our users to do. Luckily, we didn't act on that instinct quickly. Instead, we started watching what our users were doing, and we discovered that most of them didn't even care about the photo sharing site. Instead, our service turned out to be a way for our users to show their photos on sites like eBay, LiveJournal, Craigslist, and social networking sites like MySpace.

Instead of just assuming that we knew what our users were doing, we figured it out by carefully monitoring our logs and studying our analytics. Rather than tell our users they couldn't do certain things, we stepped back and decided that if this is what they love to do with our service, we should make it even easier for them to do it. That's when we started Photobucket.

Users were jumping through all kinds of technical hoops to find free sites in which they could host their photos and link to them from other sites. Most of those sites were eventually shutting down that sort of behavior, breaking images on other sites. What a pain. We created Photobucket to make this behavior that we were observing to be dead simple to do and designed the site for this one specific use case.

Users loved it! We put up a way that users could donate five dollars through Paypal, and these donations started flowing in to cover our costs of maintaining the site. You know you're on to something when the community starts donating money to make sure it stays alive.

From there, the growth of Photobucket was staggering. At one point, we were growing at about the size of one Flickr (another popular photo-sharing site) per month. We eventually sold the company to Fox Interactive Media, a division of Rupert Murdoch's News Corporation. All of this happened because we found something users loved and wanted, and then obsessively made it easier for them to do it. If you really pay attention to what your customers love, your path becomes obvious even when they're doing something you don't think you want them to be doing.

At TechStars, we're fond of telling each company to look for the one thing that you couldn't take away from your customers without them screaming at you. Once they find it, we encourage them to make that one thing even better. Photobucket is a great example of a company that did one thing really well, even though it's not what the founders initially set out to do.

TechStars 2007 company Intense Debate stumbled across their one thing, too—making blog comments great. Intense Debate originally started as a live, online, real-time debating system. It quickly morphed into the best blog-commenting system on the Web and was adopted by tens of thousands of sites. Today, Intense Debate powers comments on top sites such as United Press International (UPI) and the company was acquired in 2008 by Automattic. The founders of Intense Debate deserve tremendous credit for focusing on what their users told them to—threading blog comments and enabling bloggers to easily reply to commenters through e-mail. In this case, they found the two things their users love.

Don't Plan. Prototype!

Greg Reinacker

Greg is the founder and CTO of NewsGator Technologies, a provider of enterprise social computing software, and has been a TechStars mentor since 2007.

Over Christmas vacation in 2002, I did what every good programmer does—I threw away something that worked perfectly well and wrote my own new version. I'm referring to my blog software, which I wrote from the ground up to replace Radio Userland, the blog software I was previously using.

By January 2003 I realized I had also thrown out my RSS aggregator (which was part of the Radio Userland product) and I became painfully aware that the RSS aggregator was an important part of my routine. So, credit card in hand, I set out to find a new one with the intention of buying something quickly and then getting back to my real job, which was doing .NET consulting work.

There weren't many RSS aggregators around at the time. In fact, I think there were about four of them. None of them worked the way

I thought they should; one was close, with an Outlook look-and-feel, but the shortcut keys were totally different, so I'd end up doing things like forwarding items I meant to delete. During this exploration process a light bulb went on and I wondered why I couldn't simply read my RSS feeds inside of Outlook, where I read everything else?

I built a super-quick prototype to display some of my feeds in Outlook, took a screen shot, and posted that on my blog on January 4, 2003. Overnight there was a flurry of comments, all of them positive about the idea. Fewer than 10 days had elapsed at this point.

Encouraged by this feedback, I stayed up late one night working on my prototype, and posted a 0.1 version of the "Outlook News Aggregator" on my blog on January 5. Version 0.2 came out on the 6th, encouraging those skeptics who will never install a 0.1 version of anything, let alone something that talks to Outlook. The ninth public release, 0.9, was out on February 10, and the release of NewsGator 1.0 came on February 23, 2003. Somewhere in between all those releases I also built an e-commerce site to sell NewsGator with direct credit card processing built in. This all happened within 60 days of having the idea.

During the early development process, I was very public about discussing potential new features and how things should work. I wrote openly and asked questions on my blog about technical issues such as what the HTTP referrer should be set to when an aggregator retrieves a feed. While there were existing examples of several possible solutions, none seemed ideal. As a result, I tried to take advantage of the early adopter folks in my audience to define what the right behavior should be. Most of this was new at the time; together with a few other people, I was laying the groundwork for future applications that would use RSS.

I remember on the first day of NewsGator's release, it sold 25 copies. I sat back and did the math: 25 copies times $29 each times 365 days in the year—that was my initial business plan! One nice thing about having developed the product out in the open was that on the first day there were many blog posts and articles about it, including some from influential folks who had been using the product for a while. Most of them praised the product and talked about how it had already changed their lives, made them more attractive, and doubled their salaries. Well, at least the first part.

The next few months were spent iterating the product, mostly working on some of those difficult features that I never figured out how to do for version 1.0. I also started to notice companies ordering the product for internal business use. There were a few orders for 50 units at a time that, needless to say, were encouraging. Two months after the 1.0 release, I stopped my consulting work so I could focus full-time on NewsGator.

I decided that if I was going to strike it rich and retire on a Caribbean island, I was going to have to get the mainstream tech press to take notice of NewsGator. Having no idea how to make that happen, I decided I needed a PR representative. I asked around with some well-connected folks I knew and one of them made an introduction for me to someone who specialized in PR for small technology companies. By this point, the company was making enough money to pay her and most of the expenses, although not enough to pay me too. Ah, the life of a startup—I took one for the team and paid her instead of me. We spent a lot of time on the road, talking to press and analysts, and doing events, all of which paid off in actual coverage of the product and awareness of the company.

In January 2004 I took the wraps off the previous few months' work, which was NewsGator 2.0 and the NewsGator Online platform, allowing synchronization between multiple computers and the on-line aggregator application. It was an ambitious release for me: lots of products at the same time (mobile, other e-mail clients, and a web service), and a separate premium content services. NewsGator Online was a subscription service, starting at five dollars a month, and I had a hundred or so beta folks using the platform before its release.

The first half of 2004 was spent working on the products as well as adding new applications built on the online platform. I built a dedicated content reader for Windows Media Center Edition, which was soon featured in the Online Spotlight part of the Media Center interface. I envisioned an ecosystem of products, all synchronized together, for consuming content. It was about this time I realized I couldn't build this all by myself.

By this point, the company was earning about $20,000 per month and was growing, albeit not as quickly as I would have liked. I figured I could continue to grow the company organically, and probably make some decent money over the next year, but would likely end up getting stomped on by someone larger and better funded. An alternative was to find someone to invest some money in the company, get to work on building out the vision I had in my head, and swing for the fences.

Along with Brad Feld, who somehow deciphered what was going on from the mysterious charts and graphs I showed him, I decided to go for it. If I hadn't been prototyping and iterating aggressively, I would never have gotten to a point at which I had a chance. And five years later, I know I made the right choice, as today NewsGator is a leader in providing enterprise social computing software and employs around 100 people.

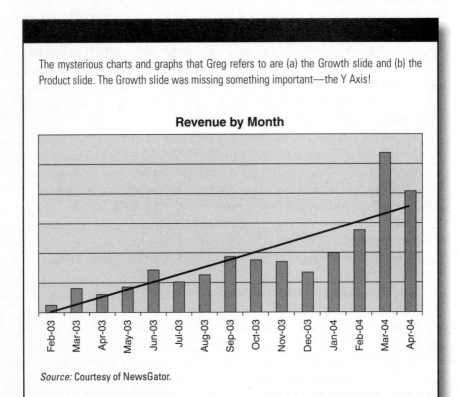

The mysterious charts and graphs that Greg refers to are (a) the Growth slide and (b) the Product slide. The Growth slide was missing something important—the Y Axis!

Revenue by Month

Source: Courtesy of NewsGator.

When Brad saw this slide, his first question was, "What's the y axis?" Greg hemmed and hawed. Brad said, "Greg—I promise I won't tell anyone—but this graph is worthless if the Y Axis is $0 to $1." Greg confessed that his March revenue was "about $20K."

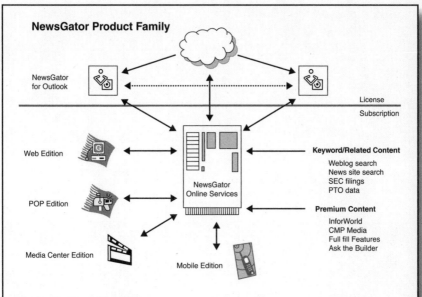

NewsGator Product Family

NewsGator for Outlook

License
Subscription

Web Edition

Keyword/Related Content
Weblog search
News site search
SEC filings
PTO data

NewsGator Online Services

POP Edition

Premium Content
InforWorld
CMP Media
Full fill Features
Ask the Builder

Media Center Edition

Mobile Edition

Source: Courtesy of NewsGator.

On the other hand, the Product slide was dynamite. This is the one that really hooked Brad.

Greg knew how to share his vision, but more importantly, he started prototyping immediately. Nothing helps to convey ideas as well as a functioning early product.

You Never Need Another Original Idea

Niel Robertson

Niel is the founder and CEO of Trada, the first PPC marketplace that allows agencies and in-house advertisers to leverage the skills of hundreds of the best PPC experts in the world, and has been a TechStars mentor since 2007.

I first gave a talk about product management at TechStars during the summer of 2008. One of the things that I said that night caught the attention of all the founders, and we ended up talking about it for hours: "As long as I listen to my customers, I never need to have another original idea."

It's a simple concept. Go get customers, then listen. It really can be that simple.

The ability to listen is an important skill for any startup founder. We're all accustomed to trying to persuade people to try our products, to invest in our companies, or to listen to what we have to say. If you're doing that with customers, you're doing it backward.

Too many startups build things that they think their customers will want. If you're looking for creative ideas that can make your company better, simply spend time with your customers. It's not rocket science, but I'm always surprised by how few companies are really good at doing this.

Trada is Niel's third startup. His first, Service Metrics, was a huge success and was acquired by Exodus for $280 million in 1999. He second, Newmerix, ultimately failed after shipping a series of products and building a modest, but not compelling, customer base. When Niel started thinking about Trada, he spent three months working closely with Brad's partner, Seth Levine, to better understand how PPC worked, where the weaknesses were, and what the end customers of PPC campaigns were struggling with. Google had pioneered a $20 billion PPC industry with AdWords, but Niel believed it was inefficient and, for many advertisers, very ineffective.

After 90 days, Niel had an enormous amount of data and a clear thesis to pursue. Foundry Group provided seed financing for Trada, but Niel wasn't done talking to customers. As the early Trada team built and released their first product, Niel infused the culture of "listening to your customers" into the fabric of Trada. Every feature, element of product design, and business decision was a result of the data coming back from their early customers.

Trada totally nailed this. They recently raised another financing led by none other than Google Ventures and at the time this chapter was written was one of the fastest-growing startups in Boulder, Colorado.

A sign seen around the TechStars office in Cambridge, Massachusetts, known as The Penthouse.

Get It Out There

Sean Corbett

Sean is one of the founders of HaveMyShift, an online service that allows shift workers to have more flexibility and freedom, and a graduate of the TechStars 2009 Boston class.

HaveMyShift is an online marketplace for the 74 million hourly workers in the United States. We allow them to trade shifts with one another, giving them options to choose a better work schedule for themselves. So far, we have helped over 5,600 employees in companies like Starbucks, Jamba Juice, Wegmans, Walmart, Ikea, Target, and Whole Foods trade over 44,000 hours of shifts.

When we started working on HaveMyShift, we consciously made an effort not to build more features than people wanted or needed. In fact, we launched the site within two weeks of the first lines of code. People have asked me how we've been able to go from idea to launch in two weeks. Well, it's because of my bike.

I didn't have a car, so I just got on my bike and rode around to several Chicago area Starbucks stores. I just started asking those employees and store managers what they wanted. I asked them what features our software would need to have for them to start using it. Not only were they excited about it, they helped me understand that if we could do one or two things well, then our software would be immediately valuable to them.

Early on, we struggled with our decision to get our half-baked product into the hands of our users so early in the development process. The biggest reason to delay releasing code has always been "What if the users don't like it and never come back?" The thought of real people having a bad experience is daunting. How would we ever get explosive growth if the product turned people off?

In companies that rely on having a large user base as ours does, it is very unlikely that you will offend enough people quickly enough to dampen your future growth. Bad news and bad experiences don't travel quickly; people just don't tell each other about services they don't get value out of. If they do, it's easy to jump in and fix their problems, which can make you a hero. Build the smallest possible product that allows you to test assumptions and answer questions about your business, and then get it out there.

Listening to your users early in the life of a product is a great way to build something that more and more people use and pay for. We quickly found out it was not a good idea to send every interested user an e-mail every time a shift in their area posted—this resulted in us being on spam blacklists within weeks of launching. We had to change our messaging model to digest e-mail only. This led us to a great way to define the free and paid features of the site. We offer an emergency shift, which sends more e-mail to more people, for a fee. We did not have experience managing retail stores but we quickly got the message from our users that managers wanted to see some form of reputation system on the site. By getting our product out there early, we found out which early features were important to our users.

Having people use HaveMyShift gave credibility to the business. Each time we added a zero to the size of our user base, we gained credibility. Having a credible story to tell helped us get in to Tech-Stars, and helped us get face time with increasingly useful people in the retail industry. Persuading people to try HaveMyShift was instrumental in getting meetings in which we landed subsequent, bigger customers. Repeating this process over and over again has served us well.

One of the classic mistakes that startups make is developing a product in the absence of customers. It's simply impossible to learn unless people are using your product. Sean's story is typical of startups that work. Instead of building what he imagined to be the perfect product, he jumped on his bicycle and visited Chicago area Starbucks stores and asked those employees and managers what would help them most. Within weeks, those same users were using a live product and giving him feedback.

HaveMyShift's early users were so passionate about the product that they were willing to look past early flaws. Those same users helped him build credibility and had a massive impact on the product and business model.

Avoid Tunnel Vision

Bijan Sabet

Bijan is a general partner at Spark Capital in Boston. He is one of the founders of TechStars in Boston, and has been a TechStars mentor since 2009.

Photo by Michael Indresano, Courtesy of Spark Capital

In the world of startups, big ideas are one thing but execution is everything. The best entrepreneurs I know execute well by doing several things.

- Develop passion and vision for the problem they are trying to solve.
- Identify and understand what they have to do to make it happen.
- Combine sheer will, determination, and focus to make it happen with a healthy sense of urgency.
- Have perspective that things rarely go as planned.

I think the first three are straightforward, but the last one can be incredibly challenging.

When I'm mentoring companies during TechStars, entrepreneurs often nail the first three items on the list, as these are the raw materials of a typical TechStars company. The difficulty is making sure that they recognize that having tunnel vision can be deadly.

Let me share a specific example. The founders of Boxee (boxee.tv)—a company I'm on the board of—have a vision and passion to bring the open Web to television. When they started the company, their vision for doing this was to develop an open source media application and tie it to a web service and a smooth user interface made for a TV remote control rather than a mouse and keyboard.

At first, they believed the best way to do this was to build a low-cost set-top box and integrate their application with the hardware. They raised a small amount of capital from friends and angel investors. They built a prototype of the hardware and software and allowed a small number of users to test the product. That was in 2007.

By 2008, they decided to seek venture capital to fund the company. When they came to see me they believed that their hardware and software experience was the right way to go. But I didn't see it that way. I suggested that they ditch the hardware and focus on the software and user experience. After my first meeting with Avner Ronan, Boxee's co-founder and CEO, I told him I loved the vision but I wanted to invest in "Un-Boxee"; basically, Boxee without the box!

I wasn't the only one who provided that feedback. They heard it from a few other VCs and a few of their trusted advisors. After a great deal of thought, the company decided to focus on software. They came to the conclusion it would be the fastest way to distribute their product and allow them to build a capital-efficient company.

While they were deliberate in this strategic change, they made the decision promptly. They then proceeded to distribute their application to hundreds of thousands of users quickly and at a low cost. They subsequently raised venture capital from my firm (Spark Capital) and Union Square Ventures.

Their user base grew quickly and Boxee was approached by a number of large consumer electronics companies about bundling the Boxee software with their consumer electronics hardware. At this point the Un-Boxee product (the software only) was receiving incredibly positive feedback, and Boxee was now in position to go back to their original idea of a hardware and software combination.

They cut the appropriate deals and are planning on releasing a combined hardware and software product (the Boxee Box) shortly.

There is still plenty of work and risk in front of the company. But they wouldn't have been able to get to this point if they had been bogged down by rigid tunnel vision. By having a perspective that not everything goes as planned, Avner and his team were able to get to a point at which they could realize their original vision for Boxee, just not necessarily on the path they had planned.

Focus

Jared Polis

Jared is one of the founders of TechStars. He is also the founder of BlueMountain Arts.com and ProFlowers, among many other companies. Jared is also currently serving as a U.S. Congressman for the second district of Colorado.

Ideas are easy to come by. I have had many that I never had time to see through and heard many other good ones from flakes and drifters, but I believe the key to success is focusing on a good idea and implementing it well. In the case of ProFlowers, my idea was to disintermediate the supply chain by sending flowers directly from the grower to the customer, delivering fresher flowers at a better price. From there, it became a matter of focusing on the implementation. I had to invent a system to get the orders to the growers. Since many flower growers were extremely low tech at the time and couldn't be relied upon for Internet access, we created a foolproof way of faxing FedEx labels directly to the growers right on sticky peel-off paper for them to affix to the boxes. We also had to become good at marketing and customer acquisition. To be the best if no one else knew about us would have meant limited success. So, after we raised capital, we hired top-notch direct marketers and became great at getting new customers. The company grew rapidly since I founded it in 1998, went public in 2004, and had over $250 million in sales when it was acquired by Liberty Media in 2006 for around $500 million.

Staying focused is critical but is one of the most difficult challenges entrepreneurs face. In ProFlowers' second year, we decided that lobsters were just like flowers; fresh from the wharf was the same as fresh from the farm. Lobsters, like flowers, had to be delivered quickly, and our technology worked perfectly with little modification. However, we didn't think through the fact that the U.S. lobster market is tiny compared to the U.S. flower market. In addition to lobsters, we decided to explore other countries such as Japan. We ended up launching a Japanese subsidiary and I even went to Japan to watch focus groups of Japanese consumers to see how their flower-purchasing habits differed from those in the United States, which we were familiar with. While culturally interesting, our foray into Japan was a complete waste of time. In retrospect, we should have focused 100 percent of our time, effort, and capital capturing what we could of the $7 billion U.S. flower market. Maybe if we were a mature billion-dollar company with a large market share in flowers we could have looked at other market opportunities. Fortunately, we reversed course quickly and limited the losses from our adventures with lobsters and Japan.

Jared is a remarkable entrepreneur. As the son of two entrepreneurs (the founders of Blue Mountain Arts, one of the largest and most enduring greeting card companies in the United States), he co-founded his first successful company—AIS—when in college and sold it to Exodus in the mid-1990s for $21 million. Working closely with his parents, he then created BlueMountainArts.com, the online version of Blue Mountain Arts. Brad and Jared became close friends after Brad moved to Boulder in 1995. In 1999, BlueMountainArts.com was acquired by Excite.com for around $800 million. Ironically, Ryan McIntyre—one of Brad's partners in Foundry Group—was one of the co-founders of Excite. Jared started ProFlowers while he was still running BlueMountainArts.com but started focusing on it 100 percent of the time after Excite acquired BlueMountainArts.com.

When David and Brad started TechStars in 2006, they approached only two other entrepreneurs to help fund the first year of the program. David's previous business partner, David Brown, was one. The other was Jared.

Jared Polis (right) and David Cohen during orientation day at TechStars in 2008.

Iterate Again

Colin Angle

Colin is the chairman, CEO, and founder of iRobot, a public company (IRBT) valued around $500 million that makes the popular Roomba vacuum cleaner robot and a series of military robots such as the Packbot. He is one of the founders of TechStars in Boston and has been a TechStars mentor since 2009.

A private mission to the moon and sale of the movie rights—this was our first business plan when we started iRobot in 1990. The surprising thing was how far we actually got. The launch vehicle (a robot named Grendel) was developed and flight-tested on a very small spacecraft affectionately called a "brilliant pebble" at Edwards Air Force base. We had agreed to sell NASA the data collected to help finance the mission. We even recruited the producer of the *Blues Brothers* movie to be on our board of directors. Although it was an interesting and bold idea, it didn't work out in the end. However, we had found a way to get paid for the effort through government programs, got to work on a very cool project, and were far from disheartened. We knew that there were going to be more innovative and unique ideas in our future, and we set out to try again. We decided to pursue industrial cleaning robots in partnership with Johnson Wax, oil exploration robots with both Baker Hughes and

Halliburton, and robot toys with Hasbro. In each of these cases we were able to enter a market with a partner willing to shoulder much of the cost, do some great work together, create value for each other, and in each of these cases, exit the relationship with both our moral and financial positions intact. Of course, none of those business plans ultimately worked out.

We were doing more than treading water during this period. We were learning what our technology was both good and not so good for. More importantly, we were learning how to run a business and how to forge successful partnerships. We learned when intellectual property matters and when it gets in the way of progress. We learned that forcing people to do what you want may work when you have your own legion of lawyers, but for the rest of us, it is the interpersonal relationships that truly matter. We learned that very few people care how you accomplish something. Instead, these people care more about whether you create value for your end user.

Finally, we learned that a mission statement does actually make a difference. Ours, "Build Cool Stuff, Deliver Great Product, Have Fun, Make Money, Change the World" kept us unified with a common purpose while gut-wrenching change surrounded us. It reminded us that our goal was to have fun and make money. Most importantly, it reminded us that our mission was not only to make money, but to change the world in the process. This is a cause worth pursuing, even if it is to call your customers to tell them that (a) no, the robot isn't done yet, and (b) please pay us anyway so we can make payroll.

A company that is well-positioned to endure the hardships encountered during the early phases of its existence gives itself time to find success. In the case of iRobot, we may have been less successful at building toys and exploring for oil, but we were able to use that experience to build high quality machines that cleaned in a cost-effective manner, with the industry's most innovative artificial intelligence software. Also, we had survived long enough to reach a point when a fledgling robot company sounded like a relatively safe investment relative to many dotcom startups of the time. We were thus able to attract VC funding.

Under these circumstances, the Roomba was funded, designed, and born on Sept 15, 2002. We would have never reached this point if we hadn't kept iterating. And the world has never been the same since.

While Colin's story ends abruptly in September 2002 with the launch of the Roomba, that's also the beginning of the next chapter of the iRobot story. Brad keeps a list titled "Companies I Regret Not Investing In." iRobot is at the top of the list, as it is now a public company with a market cap around $500 million.

Brad knew Colin from MIT—they were fraternity brothers and friends. Colin started iRobot in 1990 and was still iterating in 2002 when he spent some time at Brad's house in Eldorado Springs, just outside of Boulder, Colorado. It was a beautiful day in the incredible canyon that Brad lives in and they spent the day talking about iRobot, entrepreneurship, and investors. Brad gave Colin some suggestions about funding iRobot and in the back of his mind was privately excited about the idea of investing in the company. He knew nothing about robots, however, and when he mentioned it one of his partners at the VC firm he was part of at the time (Mobius Venture Capital) at his Monday partners meeting, it was immediately dismissed since "the Japanese will crush all the U.S. robot companies." Brad never dug in further, was happy when iRobot was funded and ultimately went public, but always secretly regretted not having more courage to step up and participate in the financing. In this case, Brad also iterated—he realized that iRobot wasn't really a "robotics company," but in the vocabulary of Foundry Group (his current VC firm), it is a "human-computer interaction" company in which the magic is really software, even though the software is developed in a mechanical device. While iRobot is on Brad's list of "Companies I Regret Not Investing In," he too learned from the experience, iterated, and doesn't think he will make that particular mistake again.

Fail Fast

Alex White

Alex is founder and CEO of Next Big Sound, a company that provides online music analytics and insights, which raised about $1 million from Foundry Group, Alsop-Louie Partners, and SoftTechVC after completing TechStars in 2009.

Photo by Rebecca Stern

After my freshman year in college, I landed an internship at Universal Records in New York City and came up with the idea for a web site that would let anyone play the role of a record mogul and sign bands to their own fantasy label. For three years, I couldn't stop thinking about it but told virtually no one. During my senior year of college, I took an entrepreneurship course and formed a team to pursue this idea. We raised a seed round of funding, launched at the end of the summer and moved back to Chicago, where my three co-founders were still seniors at Northwestern. I was supposed to start a consulting job in New York City but quit before I started to pursue the business full-time. I spent the year sleeping on couches, touring the country helping manage a band and fighting my way to registering thousands of artists and users for our fledgling service. By the spring, we had been profiled in the *New York Times,* had several small investment offers, many overqualified individuals who wanted to work at the company, and barely enough money in our bank account to pay the streaming data costs we were incurring each month. This was when we applied to TechStars.

I tell you this background only to illustrate how much had been invested in this idea. I thought we had all the answers and would be able to figure out any challenge we came across. Millions of registered users? We'll get there. Thousands of unsigned bands uploading demo tracks? We'll figure it out. But I had come to realize that even if we accomplished these goals, it wasn't clear that we had an economically viable business.

We drove a thousand miles overnight from Chicago to Boulder brainstorming ideas. We knew that the high-level concept of our first site still really inspired us. How does a band become famous? How does a band go from playing in their garage to headlining a nationwide tour? We also knew that if we wanted to have the freedom, excitement, and opportunity to run our own business, we needed to find something financially viable.

On the first day of TechStars, we decided to change our idea. Many people were surprised, but the decision was easy. We were tired of sugarcoating our status and deluding ourselves about the engagement and registration numbers. Making money off a streaming music destination site was a challenge that no longer motivated us to stay up hacking late into the night and jump out of bed every morning to start working.

We were nervous about telling our newest investors that we wanted to drop the idea we applied with until David Cohen made it clear on the first day that TechStars invests in founders, not ideas. This gave us explicit permission to fail with our initial idea without having to shut down the company and fire ourselves. At TechStars, we were given the opportunity to give it a second try.

We'd heard the statistics like everyone else. We all know that failure is the likely outcome of any individual new venture. However, with each iteration in the marketplace, you give yourself a better chance for success. You miss 100 percent of the shots you don't take. You only truly fail if you stop trying. So fail fast. Learn quickly. And start again.

Too many people take the phrase "fail fast" literally. It doesn't mean that you should make sure that your business fails fast. It means that you should be happy about having a bunch of little failures along the path to success, because if you're not failing, you're probably just not trying enough stuff.

Next Big Sound did an amazing job of failing fast. Alex and his partners woke up on the second day of TechStars and immediately began exploring several new ideas that grew out of their interest in the music industry and independent bands. At the end of the first week of the program, they started working in earnest on what turned into their music analytics product.

At first, they organized the data they were tracking in a way that band managers would find appealing, but as a result made it difficult for a typical end user to look up information on a band. After showing this early version to a number of people, they kept getting feedback that they should model their user interface after popular web analytics products like Compete and Quantcast, which tracked similar data for web sites instead of band mentions and song plays. They failed fast, scrapping their initial user interface and coming up with the one they use today.

During the summer, Alex and his partners listened attentively to all of the feedback they got, tried lots of different things, and continued to succeed by failing fast. On investor day, Alex completely nailed his presentation and Next Big Sound quickly raised a venture financing after the 2009 program ended.

Pull the Plug When You Know It's Time

Paul Berberian

Paul is a serial entrepreneur, having co-founded five companies, including Raindance Communications, which went public in 2000 and was acquired by West in 2006. He has been a TechStars mentor since 2007.

I started my fifth company in 2007. My first three companies were successful and the fourth company I started was off to a great start. So, I did what every serial entrepreneur does—I started a new one. I came up with the idea of a thing I called the "Zenie Bottle"—a beautiful, collectible physical object (similar to a Lava Lamp) linked to a social web site mash-up. I pulled the plug on the project a year later. Here is where I went wrong.

I built the business for my ego, not the market. The idea I started with was very simple: sell a novelty item that was fun to collect. The Zenie Bottle was a pretty glass bottle filled with a colorful substance that, when shaken, looked like a genie was living inside. But I didn't feel like selling a novelty item was a big enough idea, so I added elements to the business to make it more complex and hip. I attached a social web site mash-up in which the owner of a Zenie Bottle would have a virtual bottle on the Web where they could put pictures, music, and video into it so they could share it with their friends. I also created an elaborate story in the form of a serious web video of the origin of the Zenie Bottle with the goal of having the Zenie Bottle become a crossover entertainment experience. If it sounds complex, it was.

I ramped expenses before we had success in the market. If you are planning for success, that's good, but don't spend as if you are successful. I took our burn rate to more than $100,000 a month before we launched, which is fine for some businesses, but not a novelty business. All the unnecessary complexities I added, such as the web site and the video series, required us to spend the money. We quickly turned into an entertainment company, not a novelty business, well before we knew if our novelty concept made any sense.

I was embarrassed to tell people what I was doing. In hindsight, the idea was silly and didn't fit my personality. I told myself that I would be proud of my accomplishment if we had tremendous success. But that wasn't enough—I needed to be proud of what I was working on every single minute of every single day.

Ultimately, we were underfunded for the scope of our effort. We weren't sure of our identity. Were we a novelty item, a social web site mash-up, or an entertainment property? Nope—we were all three! In each category, someone other than us was already the winner. While combining all three may have worked, it would require Herculean efforts to rise above the din of other more focused companies. We were hoping to become a fad—with very little effort. While this would have been nice, it was a fantasy.

Any one of the mistakes mentioned could have been overcome, but the combination of all of them did us in. We realized our mistakes fairly early and decided that it was better to close up shop, return the remaining cash (about 20 percent of what we raised) to our investors, and sell the assets instead of thrashing around trying to reshape the business into something different.

Brad was one of the investors in the Zenie Bottle. Brad had been a seed investor in Paul's second company (Raindance) and loved working with Paul. When Paul first mentioned Zenie Bottle, Brad didn't get it, but was amused by it. Paul was so excited about it at the time that Brad committed on the spot to invest in the angel round.

When Brad saw the first prototype, he said to Paul something like "I didn't realize I had funded a bong company!" Paul ignored Brad and steered him to his computer, where he showed off all the cool ideas for the web site he was going to create.

A few months later, Brad and Paul had dinner. Paul seemed down and when confronted, admitted that the Zenie Bottle embarrassed him. It wasn't selling, no one really cared, and even he didn't really know why he was doing it anymore. Brad and Paul talked late into the night with Brad telling him much of what he had been thinking but hadn't been willing to talk about because Paul had been so enthusiastic about the idea. While it was easier for Brad to be a cheerleader and support his friend, it would have been much more valuable to Paul for Brad to say what he was thinking and feeling at the time. During the course of the evening, Brad came clean and said that he never really understood why Paul had been working on the Zenie Bottle.

A week or so after the dinner, Paul decided to pull the plug. As part of this, he decided it would be better to send the remaining money back to his investors rather than run things all the way to the end and use up all of his investors' money on something he didn't believe in. Once Paul admitted he wasn't excited about the Zenie Bottle anymore, he pulled the plug.

Now, pulling the plug, like failing fast, doesn't always mean that you shut down the company. The original vision of Paul's third company, Raindance Communications, was to create a video service on the Internet. Raindance was founded in 1996, well before Internet video was commonplace. Paul and his partners raised some initial financing, built a data center, created a streaming Internet video service, and got some initial customers. They quickly got the business up to $200,000 per month of revenue before hitting a wall and realizing that to build a substantial business they needed to do a number of things very differently. They were also frustrated with the customers and the market dynamics, as the amount of noise around Internet video was substantial, making it difficult for Raindance to stand out from all of the other offerings.

So they pulled the plug. They stepped back from what they had created and thought about what they could do better than anyone else in the world. As part of their Internet video business, they were working with audio conferencing technology with the idea of incorporating audio conferencing into Internet video in some way. They realized one day that there was a much bigger opportunity in transforming the way audio conferencing worked. Up to this point, audio conferencing was expensive, required human intervention in the form of an operator, and was impossible to control over the Internet. Paul and his partners decided to build on the technology and data center infrastructure they had created for their Internet video service and use it for a reservationless conferencing service.

Over the next several years, Raindance Communication built an $80 million company that helped make audio conferencing commonplace and affordable. Also, they were an early entrant in the web collaboration market, took the company public, became profitable, and were eventually acquired by a much larger company. By pulling the plug on the first incarnation of Raindance, Paul and his partners ended up creating a valuable company.

In the summer of 2009, Paul Berberian talks about the failure of Zenie Bottle.

THEME 2: PEOPLE

The famous real estate cliché is "The three most important things in real estate are location, location, location." An analogous entrepreneurship cliché is "the three most important things in entrepreneurship are people, people, people."

At TechStars, everything starts with people. We deliberately describe TechStars as "a mentorship-driven startup accelerator" since the mentors are a fundamental component of what makes TechStars special. The entrepreneurs who participate in TechStars are equally important, but we think one without the other is like cookies without milk, or chocolate without peanut butter, or—well—you get the idea.

People come in all shapes and sizes, have many different experiences, and a wide variety of perspectives. One of our goals with TechStars is to expose first-time entrepreneurs to a wide range of these people. And, as a special bonus, we expose the more experienced mentors to a variety of fresh perspectives from the entrepreneurs they work with. Both entrepreneurs and mentors participate and both benefit.

Over the course of the three-month long TechStars program, lifelong friendships are formed. The friendships happen between founders, entrepreneurs and mentors, and even among the mentors themselves. People are at the core of every community and TechStars is no exception.

Don't Go It Alone

Mark O'Sullivan

Mark is the founder and CEO of Vanilla, which makes forum software that is used to power discussions on more than 300,000 sites across the Web. Vanilla raised $500,000 after completing Tech-Stars in 2009.

Before TechStars, all of the work I did on Vanilla was done alone. While I had the members of the Vanilla community helping me with features and bugs, all new initiatives were mine and all final decisions were made by me. If I decided not to do anything, nothing got done. When I first spoke with David Cohen, he immediately stressed the importance of having at least one co-founder. Having been working alone for so long, I really didn't understand why he felt it was so important. I was absolutely positive that I'd be fine on my own, and in retrospect, I couldn't have been more wrong.

When I set out to find a co-founder, my list of candidates was very short. I needed someone whom I could trust implicitly, had the skills and dedication to do the work, and who I would work well with. These requirements brought the list down to two people. One person was working at Microsoft in Seattle and had just bought a house. He simply couldn't afford to quit working and try to start up a new company. The other person was single, had money saved in the bank, and was coming to the end of a consulting contract. All I needed to do was convince him.

I met Todd Burry over 10 years ago in Toronto at the first tech company I worked for where he was the head of the web development department. Todd immediately disliked me because I looked remarkably similar to his high school nemesis. Despite this fact, we became fast friends and worked closely over the years. Todd was incredibly smart and helped me become a better programmer. A number of years after leaving that company, working at Microsoft, and eventually returning to Toronto as a contract programmer, I reconnected with Todd and we began sharing contracts and working together again. I knew we worked well together and I had absolute confidence in his skills as a developer and his mind for business. To put it bluntly, Todd is just way smarter than I am.

They say that the first cut is the deepest, and cutting my ownership of Vanilla in half should have been a tough pill to swallow, but it really wasn't. It took a number of lengthy phone calls, some code review of Vanilla 2 so he could get up to speed, and introductions to David Cohen at TechStars, but Todd eventually agreed to come on board.

When TechStars began, Todd and I would return to our shared accommodations each night and reflect on the day. We thought it was exhausting in the beginning of the summer and I'm so glad we had no idea of how much more difficult it would get. Ignorance is, most certainly, bliss. I cannot count the number of times I would reflect on a day and think to myself, "There's no way I could have gotten through that day alone." By the end of the summer, there was no longer any personal time available—Todd and I worked 14-hour-plus days, every single day of the week.

In the 2009 TechStars group, there was one company that had a lone founder. It was painfully obvious to me, watching the lone founder struggle to make progress, what could have happened had I not brought Todd on board with Vanilla. At the opposite end of the spectrum, I watched a company with four co-founders continually knock it out of the park and wished I had added a third person to the Vanilla founding team.

It wasn't that I truly couldn't have done it by myself (I think I could have). Instead, it was that I would have missed so much. Todd and I were able to split up tasks: if there was development work to be done, one of us could stay behind and do it while the other attended meetings or talks; if we were both in on meetings, I knew that he was grasping things that were slipping past me, and vice versa. To be able to reflect and share our thoughts on each day was the true value that I discovered in having a co-founder, and that is something that lives on well beyond our time at TechStars.

Creating a company is really hard and there is way more work than you can even begin to grasp. Having someone to share your burden, walk side by side with you into battle, and sing you show tunes when you're feeling blue is invaluable.

While there are examples of companies created by single founders, many of the most successful tech companies have been created by at least two co-founders. Google (Brin and Page), Yahoo! (Yang and Filo), Apple (Jobs and Wozniak), Intel (Moore and Noyce), HP (Hewlett and Packard)—the list goes on and on. Brad's first company—Feld Technologies—was started by two people (Brad and Dave Jilk) as was David's first company, Pinpoint Technologies (both founders were named David—now that's confusing.) Even though TechStars is often associated with just David, there were four co-founders—David, Brad, David Brown (David's co-founder at Pinpoint Technologies), and Jared Polis. Entrepreneurship is a group sport—don't go it alone.

A surprise night out to Red Rocks Amphitheater to see the movie *Office Space* during the summer of 2009.

Avoid Co-Founder Conflict

Dharmesh Shah

Dharmesh is the founder and CEO of HubSpot, a provider of inbound marketing software, and the curator of the popular OnStartups blog and community. He has been a TechStars mentor since 2009.

Acommon reason for startup fatalities, particularly in the early days, is some sort of conflict between co-founders. One of the main reasons for co-founder conflict is that many aspects of the relationships were either ill-defined or misunderstood. To minimize the chance of this, it's critical that you and your co-founders come to agreement on some key issues. I've framed the most important of these as a set of questions that the co-founders should be asking each other as they enter into the business relationship. Many of these questions are hard but they get only harder with time. The sooner you address them, the better off your startup will be.

How should we split the equity? While there can be different aspects to this, the basic question is really simple: Who gets what percentage of the company? There are different schools of thought on how to arrive at an equitable answer. A perennial favorite is to decide that each founder should own an equal share. Or, you could try to come up with some formula that uses a bunch of different factors such as experience, market value, contribution to date, and expected contributions in the future. However you do it, the important thing is to decide it up front and not put off the discussion.

How will decisions get made? This is often tied to the number of shares, but not necessarily. You can have voting and non-voting shares. You can set up a board. You'll need to decide what kinds of decisions the board makes, and which ones it won't. Common areas to address are decisions around capitalization, executive hiring and firing, share issuance (dilution), and acquisitions.

What happens if one of us leaves the company? Although it may seem like a bad idea to be talking about this when you're starting the company—it's not. In the evolution of any startup, there will be good times and bad times and there will likely be times when one or more co-founders are simply not happy and not committed. You should decide how to treat this situation early when it is easier and everyone is at least semi-rational and optimistic about their future involvement in the company. The last thing the company needs is a co-founder who is no longer engaged but is hanging around out of guilt or ambiguity. Or worse, one that claims equity that you don't believe is due.

Can any of us be fired? By whom? For what reasons? Yes, that's right—even co-founders can be terminated. Too many people mix the notion of being a shareholder in a startup and having an operating role. These two things should be thought of as separate and distinct. The company should have a mechanism for gracefully terminating the operating role of a co-founder if that's the right thing to do. This is never fun but it should be discussed up front.

What are our personal goals for the startup? Although this can change over time, it's helpful to at least get a sense of what each of the co-founders wants to get from the company. If you have one co-founder who wants to build a sustainable business that is spinning off cash and run it forever and another one who wants to shoot for high growth with some type of massive exit through a sale to a much larger company, it's better to get that out in the open early and talk it through.

Will this be the primary activity for each of us? Co-founder conflict can stem from misunderstandings around how committed everyone is. Will one of the co-founders be keeping a day job until the company gets off the ground? Will one be working on another sideline business? Under what circumstances will someone decide that they just can't commit to the business full time anymore; for example, if the founders have to go without a salary for six months.

What part of our plan are we each unwilling to change? Not all startups need to change their plans during the course of their evolution; just the ones that want to survive and succeed! However, there may be elements of the plan that you don't want to change. This might relate to the product being built or the market being addressed. For example, if one of the founders is fanatically obsessed with wanting to create a consumer software company that lots of people know about, then friction may be created if the model needs to shift to more of an enterprise product.

What contractual terms will each of us sign with the company? One of the best examples of this is a noncompete agreement. Will each of the co-founders be signing some sort of contract with the company beyond the shareholder agreement? If so, what are the terms of this agreement? At a minimum, all founders should be willing to assign whatever they develop to the company.

Will any of us be investing cash in the company? If so, how is this to be treated? It is very likely that one or more co-founders will be putting in some cash in the early stages of the company. It is critical to decide up front how this cash will be treated. Is it debt? Is it convertible debt? Does it buy a different class of shares? What happens if the company raises follow-on funding?

What will we pay ourselves? Who gets to change this in the future? This can be a touchy issue. Risk tolerance varies by individual and it is a good idea to factor this into determining the compensation plan for the founders. The issue can be clouded sometimes when one of the founders is investing significant cash into the enterprise.

What are the financing plans for the company? Will the company be self-funded and bootstrapped? Raise angel funding? Raise venture capital funding? What happens if this doesn't occur?

While I'm sure there are other issues that could generate co-founder conflict, you'll decrease your chances of misunderstandings and implosion of the team if you visit each of the issues identified here early in the life of your startup.

During the first few days of every TechStars cycle, we tell the 10 bright-eyed new teams that one of them will not be together at the end of the program. Unfortunately, we have not been wrong yet.

Over and over again, we see team issues with startups, especially with those composed of first-time entrepreneurs. On Day One, everyone is excited, enthusiastic, and aligned about creating something new and amazing. Several months later, one or more of the founders leave because of irreconcilable differences.

One of the biggest reasons is not addressing the issues Dharmesh describes. It's easy to talk about ideas, visions, and the product. It's hard to talk about equity splits, how much money you need to make it through each month, and your personal pressures. It's even harder to talk about the doubts you are having about your partner or the path the business is going down.

If you assume that you will have many ups and downs along the way, spending time addressing many of these issues in the first month sets the tone for the rest of the business. When something material arises, the co-founders should be willing and able to discuss the issues openly with a goal of quickly reaching consensus on how to resolve them.

Hire People Better than You

Will Herman

Will is an angel investor and entrepreneur. He is one of the founders of TechStars in Boston and has been a mentor since 2009.

> *If each of us hires people who are smaller than we are, we shall become a company of dwarfs. But if each of us hires people who are bigger than we are, we shall become a company of giants.*
>
> —David Ogilvy

You've worked your asses off, had some success and have decided it's time to start expanding your team. Surprisingly, this turns out to be one of the most difficult tasks that startups take on. Some do it too fast, hiring the first cool person they meet without thinking of the big picture. Others, painfully, wait forever until they find someone who not only meets every preconceived criterion, but can also turn water into wine. Both are common mistakes but are not nearly as problematic as the biggest hiring mistake entrepreneurs can make—hiring those less capable than themselves.

There's an old adage that A-players hire A-players while B-players hire C-players. This refers to the notion that while great performers prefer to be among high-performing people who are similar to or better than they are, mediocre (and poor) performers often want to avoid having their weaknesses exposed and their efforts and abilities challenged. As a result, they often hire people who don't threaten them.

While this is frequently the case, it misses the point. One doesn't have to be an A-player to hire an A-player; one simply has to want to succeed, have a grasp of the big picture, and have the self-confidence to hire someone better than they are. In fact, this is true when A-players are doing the hiring as well. Even they should be looking for people better than themselves, or A-plus players.

Here are some reasons why you want to hire people who are better than you:

- You can learn from those who are better, those who know more, or have done it before. Learning is a total blast—why wouldn't you want to have a blast?
- Every day people who have skills that you don't have will challenge you to develop, expand, and enhance your own set of skills.
- Great teams of people move much faster than teams of weak people, as great people feed off of each other. You want your company to do more faster, right? Time is always against you in a startup.
- Knowledge grows exponentially. The more your team knows, the more they can learn and ultimately will know.
- Better people are easier to manage and are more self-directed. Would you rather spend your time leading your company or with your head down in the trenches?

Say you're an athlete whose individual performance is key—such as a runner, cyclist, tennis player, or golfer. Do you want to train with someone worse than you? Do you get any better when you do? Of course not, you only get better when you're challenged and taught by others who are better than you are.

Hiring people more capable than you are can be scary. Will they show me up? Will they make me feel bad about how I'm doing? Will others think they're more qualified than I am to do my job? The simple answer is no.

Hiring people better than you reflects positively on you. It's a fundamental skill in managing a company, whether it's a startup or an international conglomerate. The better you are at it, the better you will be perceived as a leader and manager. Also, remember that you are the entrepreneur. You demonstrate your strong leadership ability, insane work habits, and fanatical drive every day. Those qualities can't be readily usurped. Ultimately, think of it this way: you are the hero when the organization is successful because you made it successful by building the best team.

Everyone has insecurities that they want to keep buried, and many entrepreneurs question whether people who are better than they are will expose their weaknesses. You should break through this type of thinking. Hiring great people not only makes you and the perception of you better, it makes your entire team better and drastically improves your chances for success.

This is one of the most difficult things for a first-time entrepreneur to learn to do well. After the founders, the first few employees set the tone for the company. If they are awesome, you will be off to a good start. But if one of them isn't, it'll drag everyone down.

This is another case in which great mentors can be extremely helpful. At TechStars, we encourage all of the entrepreneurs to use their mentors to help them with both recruiting and screening new employees. In many cases, the mentors have a better understanding of the strengths and weaknesses of the founders and can help evaluate new hires more effectively. Furthermore, the mentors usually have a lot more experience hiring people, so their evaluation skills and processes are more refined.

Getting the best possible people on your team makes a huge difference in the success of a company. Don't forget to use all of the resources available to you—especially your experienced mentors—to help you accomplish this.

Hire Slowly, Fire Quickly

Matt Blumberg

Matt is the founder and CEO of Return Path, a company that provides e-mail deliverability services, and he has been a TechStars mentor since 2009.

In software and service companies, people are everything. It's not just that they come first. They come first, second, and third. The earlier stage the company, the more critical each incremental new person is. Think about it—if you have 10 people in your company and you are hiring a new person, you are adding 9 percent to your workforce in one shot! You're also hiring someone who will very likely have an impact on how the DNA of your organization develops since it's still embryonic in the first few years, even if it is dominated by strong-willed founders.

When a startup decides it needs to hire a new person, it wants to hire them right this second. And when it has hired the person, the startup is loath to let them go if they aren't working out because they think they need them so badly. This creates two related temptations to avoid as you build out your team.

Temptation 1: Hiring too quickly. Just having a warm body in that open job that you need filled immediately doesn't get the job done. When you are hiring such a big percentage of your workforce, you have to have a super-high success rate. At Return Path, we have sometimes left critical jobs open for months as we cycle through candidates looking for "the one." As painful as it has been for us to limp along with the position open, taking our time and hiring the absolutely right person has always been the right decision.

It is said that with knowledge workers, the best employee is 10 times more productive and impactful than the average employee. Why settle for anything less than the absolute best?

Temptation 2: Firing too slowly. Everyone's heard the analogy about a bad employee being like a cancer in an organization—his poor performance or attitude spread and he needs to be cut out to preserve the rest of the organization. To build on this metaphor, I've always said that hiring a new person, especially an early one, is like doing an organ transplant. Even if you think there's a good match, you need to see if the body accepts or rejects the transplant, and you find out pretty quickly.

At Return Path, we always do a comprehensive 90-day performance and 360-degree review of every new or promoted employee and we aren't afraid to part ways with someone who isn't working out after 90 days in a new job. While it can feel harder to remove a new employee who isn't working out, it's almost always better to make a clean break and try again as the effort to "fix the person" is likely greater than the time and effort to hire a better person, especially when time is your most precious resource.

This advice holds no matter what level the new hires are, though the more senior the hire, the more emphatic I am about the point. Build the best possible team for your startup—even if it costs you more time than you want.

Brad still remembers the first person he fired and recalls that it took him much too long to do it. His first company, Feld Technologies, had grown to a dozen people. A few people had left the company voluntarily but no one had ever been fired. Feld Technologies was a tight, cohesive team—except for one person.

From the very beginning, this person didn't fit in to the company. Everyone else cared about the quality of the work; she didn't. People stayed late to get things finished. She didn't. People respected each other and their clients; she made fun of everyone behind their backs. People ate lunch together and generally liked to hang out. She went out to lunch with friends of hers from other companies and never socialized. When someone needed help, others jumped in. She stayed to herself. Most importantly, everyone else seemed to love what they did even when it was really challenging; she just viewed it as a job and did the minimum she needed to do to get by.

For months, Brad and his partner agonized over this. They tried to help the person, they made excuses for her performance, and rationalized the situation as "just the way it was." Down deep inside, they knew she wasn't working out, but they were afraid to take action. During this time, Brad went on a weekend-long retreat called Birthing of Giants with about 60 other entrepreneurs under the age of 40. As he talked to his new peers—many of whom were much more experienced than he was (Brad was one of the youngest at 23 years old)—a common refrain came up: "Fire her Monday." The feedback was unambiguous.

When Brad returned from the retreat he talked to his partner and they decided to fire her the first thing the following Monday. Brad remembers tossing and turning all weekend, terrified of the encounter. He woke up very early and was in the office by 7 A.M. ready to go. By 10 A.M., she still hadn't shown up. Around lunchtime, Brad got a phone message that she wasn't coming in until Tuesday because she wasn't yet back from a trip she had taken with friends over the weekend.

On Tuesday, after another restless night, Brad arrived at the office again around 7 A.M. This time she eventually showed up around 9:30. Brad went into her office and started with the punch line: he told her things weren't working out, and that he had decided to ask her to leave the company. She didn't look surprised, took a minute to pack up her stuff, said goodbye, and walked out the door. She'd clearly been fired before.

Brad then called a company meeting, something he never did because he didn't believe in company meetings at the time. The remaining 11 people gathered around the conference table while Brad nervously announced what he had done. The was a moment of silence immediately followed by one of Feld Technologies' brightest and funniest software engineers asking "Can I have her chair?" That broke the ice; not surprisingly, everyone knew this person hadn't been working out and were watching Brad and his partner to see if and when they would eventually fire her.

That day made Brad, and his company, a lot better.

If You Can Quit, You Should

Laura Fitton

Laura is the founder and CEO of oneforty, a Twitter apps marketplace, and the author of Twitter For Dummies. *Oneforty raised $2.35 million from Flybridge Capital Partners, after completing TechStars in 2009.*

I'll admit it; I'm addicted to my company.

I started oneforty as a 38-year-old single mom with no technology management background. I had never built software before in my life. In fact, I felt so thoroughly unqualified to pursue the opportunity that I started making phone calls to people that I thought could build the company for me. I simply wanted to see it come to life and I thought the best way was to recruit someone else to carry out the vision so that I could be an advisor to the company.

I had two very young, cute, reasonable excuses (my kids) why it was a bad idea for me to do a startup. I had no co-founder and I knew better than to do it alone. I tried to give the idea away and to get another group to do it. And when that failed, I quit. Well, at least I tried to quit.

I spent another four months trying creative new ways to quit the idea. I kept trying to find someone else to do it because I didn't want to do it myself. But no matter how hard I tried, I just couldn't quit.

I like to tell other founders that you have to be so stuck on your idea that you literally can't even quit. There are going to be a thousand times in the process that you're going to want to quit, so if you're going to quit it's smarter to do it sooner rather than later. If you can quit, you certainly should.

Even if you're really into your startup idea, try to quit now anyway. And if you are able to quit, do it. In my case, I was so obsessed with the idea for oneforty that I literally couldn't quit. I had to see it come to light.

If you can't quit no matter how hard you try, then you have a chance to succeed.

Amazing entrepreneurs are like forces of nature—they are unstoppable. Laura fits this description perfectly. The first time Brad met her was several years ago at the Defrag Conference. Everyone knew who @pistacio was and she couldn't stop talking about all the incredible things you could do with Twitter. While this might not be a big deal today, at the time Twitter was only being used by a limited number of techies and the phrase "social media marketing" hadn't yet been created.

Laura Fitton and team oneforty at TechStars in Boston during the summer of 2009.

Laura just stayed with it. When she applied to TechStars, she was a solo founder. We told her that her chance of success as a solo founder was low. She didn't care—she said she'd figure it out. She didn't have a technical co-founder. She told us that it was not an issue—she'd recruit someone quickly. By this point, we had no ability to quit Laura—she'd hooked us. Today, she has a great team, strong investors, and is off to a great start with oneforty. It's a good thing she didn't quit.

Build a Balanced Team

Alex White

Alex is the founder and CEO of Next Big Sound, a company that provides online music analytics and insights, which raised about $1 million from Foundry Group, Alsop-Louie Partners, and SoftTechVC after completing TechStars in 2009.

Photo by Rebecca Stern

I wish I were good at programming but I'm not. If I put the time in I could probably be good at it, but I don't enjoy it at all. Instead, I handle the business side of things for Next Big Sound. Before coming to TechStars, I always seemed to find myself surrounded by really smart people with great ideas and no way to execute them.

From my experience, interaction between technical and non-technical entrepreneurs is often minimal. When I showed up at TechStars, I found the tables completely turned as I was one of the least competent developers out of 30 founders—they had me surrounded!

I think that at the earliest stages of a company it's foolish to have more than one non-technical co-founder. For an example, think about a non-technical small business such as an auto mechanic, sandwich shop, or tailor. On one side of the equation is the actual product or service that makes money such as fixing engines, making sandwiches, or sewing clothes. On the other side is everything else that gets in the way of making money but still needs to be done; things like renting a garage, keeping the counter clean, and purchasing thread and other supplies.

As the non-technical co-founder, I view my role on the team as everything on the non-technical side of the equation, which entails things such as renting office space, raising money, paying the bills, and setting up schedules, lunches, and travel. I also have the connections and domain expertise for our particular industry so I'm focused on making sure that what we're building is valuable. I also sell what we've built.

I think that the healthiest startups have overlaps in key areas. My co-founders David Hoffman and Samir Rayani don't have to spend time helping me set up our payroll system or handling questions from our lawyers, as every minute they spend doing something I can cover myself is essentially wasted. However, I want them to be included in things like sitting in on meetings with early customers, handling direct feedback from users, and meeting with high-level investors, as they have valuable and unique contributions to these activities.

Finding a co-founder to complement your skill set is difficult and I believe it involves a strong element of luck. I had the idea for the first version of the Next Big Sound site for three years before finding my co-founders who could actually bring the site to life. Programmer-types and business-types I know run in separate circles. I can't believe that the guys I work with can stare at code all afternoon and they can't believe that I can have back-to-back phone calls for a week straight having what often seems like the very same conversation.

The real magic in our team has been growing into overlapping and complementary roles. While we were lucky to find each other, we also work really hard at this, regularly talking about how we are spending our time and whether or not our efforts overlap in effective or worthless ways. While we don't always achieve perfect balance, we are always working on it and get better all the time.

Observing Alex throughout his summer at TechStars, we discovered that he had many subtle and rare leadership qualities. One of them was that he knew how to stay out of the way of his technical team. He trusted them implicitly so he didn't over-manage them, and he balanced the team by spending much of his time clearing roadblocks for them so that they could be more efficient.

Sometimes Alex took this to extremes. During the summer of 2009 while Next Big Sound was in TechStars, the founders all lived together. Before there was a product to sell or customers to work with, Alex handled details such as paying rent, doing maintenance, shopping for food, and leading chatty visitors away from the office. While these are not your typical CEO duties, Alex felt that it was more important for his co-founders to be writing code during TechStars than dealing with distractions.

In addition to creating leverage for his technical co-founders, they also learned to trust him with a wide variety of activities that would have otherwise wasted their time.

Startups Seek Friends

Micah Baldwin

Micah is the CEO of Graphic.ly, a social digital distribution platform for comic book publishers and fans. Micah has been a TechStars mentor since 2007 and joined Graphic.ly after the company participated in TechStars in 2009. The company went on to raise $1.2 million from DFJ Mercury, Starz Media, Chris Sacca, and others.

Photo Courtesy of Renee Blodgett, MagicSauceMedia.com

Salespeople sell. It's what they do. Have you ever seen the play (or the movie) *Glengarry Glen Ross?* Salespeople sell. Want the pink Cadillac? Sell. Want the Glengarry leads? Sell. Don't sell? You're fired. It's really that simple.

In sales, the process is focused on having the salesperson win. The salesperson cannot think in any other way since his only purpose in life is to sell. For a salesperson, the customer's only reason to exist is to buy. While there is much discussion about the importance of the relationship, the relationship's only importance is to allow the salesperson to continue to sell. It's not evil—it's just how it works.

However, this doesn't work for early stage startups. The sale is not what is important. In early stage startups, the relationship reigns supreme. Why? Because startups screw up a lot. If you have solid relationships, there is an allowance for failure.

Take Lijit Networks, the last startup I worked for before becoming CEO at Graphic.ly. Lijit provides a search widget for publications that aggregates social content for individual sites and multisite content for a publisher network, and then makes it searchable. Early on, we brought on a publisher network that tripled our monthly page views. Despite the hardware we purchased and the code we wrote, the additional page views slowed down our search results, in some cases drastically. However, because we had developed solid relationships with the 1,000 publishers we had at the time, they stuck with us, as did our new publisher network. As a result, not a single customer uninstalled our service.

How did we do it? We built a relationship with each member of our community. It didn't take much; an e-mail here, a tweet there, a regular update about what was going on with our service. Our newest customer worked with us to find ways to reduce the strain on our system. We worked hard at it and established even stronger relationships with our publishers.

Recently, we brought on another new publisher network that quadrupled our traffic. In this case, there wasn't a bump. Not even a wiggle. Everything worked smoothly. How did we land this new publisher network? An earlier one—the one that tripled our previous traffic—recommended us!

When two-way relationships are developed where there is real value derived on both sides, the ability for both partners to learn from each other and grow together multiplies dramatically.

Salespeople hunt pink Cadillacs. Startups seek friends.

Many first-time entrepreneurs are afraid to sell. Others have sales backgrounds and view everything as a potential sale. Micah's statement that "startups seek friends" is an important and unique way to think about sales in a startup context.

If you are an entrepreneur who is either afraid to sell or doesn't like to sell, recognize that your goal at the beginning of your company isn't actually to sell stuff. It's to make friends. You are trying to find as many people as possible who want to be friends with your company, who care about what you are doing, and who want to help you. Long before you have anything to sell, you'll have made a bunch of new friends, all of whom are ready and eager to help you succeed.

If you are naturally a salesperson, recognize that at the beginning of your company you really don't have much to sell other than your vision. People are rarely going to pay you for your vision, but they will become your friend and spend time with you if they are inspired by your vision.

Focus on making friends first. Then remember to treat them that way. You'll have plenty of time to hunt for pink Cadillacs.

Engage Great Mentors

Emily Olson

Emily is the co-founder of Foodzie, an online marketplace where consumers can discover and buy food directly from small artisan producers. Foodzie raised $1 million from First Round Capital, SoftTech VC, Tim Ferriss, and several other angel investors after completing TechStars in 2008.

Starting a company is the hardest thing I've done in my life. It's like I'm walking into a final exam every day that is composed of essay questions on topics I've never studied. That's the reality for most entrepreneurs. Now imagine walking into that same test, but now it's multiple choice and you have someone who already took the same test sitting next to you who is telling you the answer is probably "a" or "b." That's how much easier business gets when you get the help of a great mentor.

When my Foodzie co-founders Rob LaFave, Nik Bauman, and I first arrived at TechStars, we went gangbusters on setting up meetings with any TechStars mentor who would give us the time. At the beginning of TechStars, we were in the business of meeting mentors. But then we realized that while we needed to engage mentors, we also had a business to run.

Mentors should fit into your business, which means at any given time you should only be working with a few, but their experience should match up with the challenges you face. We found that when it came to finding the right mentor, the more specific the better. As we crafted our business model early on, we worked with a pricing strategist who helped us avoid an amateur mistake that would have been difficult to fix later on. Later in the business as our team grew, we engaged a technical mentor to help us with the hiring process to not only coach us on best practices, but to help conduct technical interviews with candidates who had more experience than we would have been able to evaluate on our own.

Sure, you could probably test out an educated guess or read a book to learn some of these things, but once you're done executing on what a book tells you to do, you can't come back to the book and share how that advice was applied to your business, what worked, and what was an utter failure. Mentors love this part, as it's a two-way street—they both hear what you learn from your experiences as well as learn new things themselves.

Mentors get involved in a business for a variety of reasons. They might be passionate about the market you are going after. They might be interested in becoming a formal advisor or an early investor in your business. Or maybe they are simply one of those crazy entrepreneurs who are addicted to the startup environment and thrive off the interactions with enthusiastic, innovative, and smart entrepreneurs. Whatever their motivation is, it's your job to figure that out and try to fulfill it for the mentor, just as their job is to give you good advice.

Part of managing the relationship means figuring out how best to communicate with your mentor. We've tried a bunch of different ways and it turns out that you need to tailor what works to each individual mentor. We've tried sending weekly e-mails, setting up a private blog with daily and weekly updates, chatting over the phone, or working together live and in person. Different things work for different people—be flexible and tune it to their needs.

Make sure that you continually close the loop when you work with a mentor. The initial discussion with mentors about a particular topic is like the beginning of a really good story. Make sure you keep them posted on all the juicy details of what you are doing with their advice, as well as whatever conclusions or resolutions you come to. It sucks to not hear the ending of a story, which is how the mentor will feel if you don't close the loop.

There are so many days when I wake up thinking I have no idea what I am doing. It's no surprise that statistics show that 9 out of 10 businesses fail. For the 10 percent of businesses that do succeed, I've got a good gut feeling that solid mentorship is a part of the secret sauce.

It's possible that no one in the history of TechStars did a better job of engaging their mentors than Foodzie. Years later, Emily and the gang at Foodzie still do a great job of leveraging more experienced people around them. You never feel like you're wasting your time when you try to help Foodzie. They'll always let you know that they've put real thought into your feedback and ideas. They won't always take the advice (also smart!) but they'll always carefully consider it and close the feedback loop.

About a year after they finished with TechStars, David was advocating a "brilliant" idea to Foodzie. He thought that they should send gift baskets of Foodzie goodies to local businesses, and view it as a marketing expense. David thought that the re-orders would lead to long-term customer retention. Rob and Emily carefully considered the idea and did a couple of quick and dirty experiments. They quickly came back to David and told him that this wasn't something that they were going to pursue because their early tests gave them confidence that this wouldn't have the intended consequences. Among other issues, the receptionists were simply eating the goodies! Foodzie did a great job of closing the feedback loop and David and Foodzie learned something together in the process.

Emily Olson and Team Foodzie During TechStars in 2008.

Define Your Culture

Greg Gottesman

Greg is a managing director of Madrona Venture Group. He's one of the founders of TechStars in Seattle and serves as a mentor in the program.

Photo by Randy Stewart, blog.stewtopia.com

During the last decade, I have been convinced that the three most important factors in determining the success of a startup are the team, the product or service, and the market (timing, size, and so on). Take an A-plus entrepreneur, with a great idea for a new product or service, at the right time, and about as fast as you can tweet Susan Boyle, you'd have a success brewing.

I recently added one factor to the must-have list: the right startup culture. In other words, add a dose of bad culture to a team of superstars, a killer product, and a good market opportunity, and the result is almost always death by a thousand backstabs.

What defines a great startup culture?

Justice Potter Stewart's "I know it when I see it" standard seems particularly apt here, but not actionable.

I've attempted to define the characteristics of a great startup culture. I was aiming for a top 10 but ended up with a baker's dozen (because in life it's hard to beat a free bagel.)

1. *No politics.* In great startup cultures, everybody is giving everybody else credit. Ideas are judged on the merits, not on who came up with them. People feel comfortable that they will get their due. In not-so-great startup cultures, everyone wants to make sure everybody else knows what he or she did, even if he or she didn't do it.

2. *It's not a job, it's a mission.* Redfin's CEO Glenn Kelman likes to talk about how invigorating it can be once you realize that you don't have to be doing what you are doing. Great startup cultures are composed of people who could be doing a hundred other things, but actually choose to work themselves silly over the particular product or service their company is building. These cultures are often centered around the belief that the company is working on something important.

3. *Intolerance for mediocrity.* Great startup cultures are psychically rewarding for A-players and thoroughly awful for those who are not pulling their weight. Instead of performing to the least common denominator, great startup cultures quickly reject those who are not meeting a high bar. Those who remain revel in the fact that they are surrounded by colleagues who are as good or, in many cases, better than they are.

4. *Watching pennies.* Great startup cultures make every dollar count. Expenses are viewed with the same kind of discretion as they are on the home front. The beauty of the Amazon.com making-doors-into-desks tradition was not that it was cheaper (it probably wasn't), but rather the mentality that it engendered that Amazon was a place that didn't waste money on fancy furniture. In its early days, Intrepid Learning Solutions used to give out "Scrappy Awards" to employees who demonstrated superhuman abilities to save money. The CEO won one for renting a U-Haul and personally picking up and then moving in a free conference table from a local company that was moving. A cost-conscious attitude can be cool and, in great startup cultures, contagious.

5. *Equity-driven.* Great startup cultures create a sense that everyone on board is building something significant, an enterprise

that will be valuable in the long term. Employees want a piece of that future. Less optimal cultures are focused almost entirely on short-term cash incentives. That's not to say that short-term cash incentives are always bad; in fact, in many cases, they can be helpful in driving toward short-term goals. But when employees are focused solely on cash and not the least bit interested in equity, that's a sign that they may have lost faith in the business.

6. *Perfect alignment.* Great startup cultures are well aligned. The strategy makes sense and is aligned with the vision. People are doing what they are good at and in the right roles. Every employee, from the CEO to the office manager, is on the same page.

7. *Good communication, even in bad times.* Transparent communication is a hallmark of a great startup culture. No one is confused about the vision and where the company is headed. Communication is open and free-flowing. Hard issues are addressed directly, not ignored. Every startup goes through ups and downs. The tendency is to not want to share bad news. It's not as much fun. In great startup cultures, communication to all stakeholders actually increases during the down times.

8. *Strong leadership.* The founder of a startup should be the "cultural soul" of the company. A good leader takes that responsibility seriously and leads by example. I love this quote in David McCullough's book *Truman* by former secretary of state and army general George Marshall about the importance of leading by example and maintaining a positive attitude. "Gentleman, enlisted men may be entitled to morale problems, but officers are not. I expect all officers in this department to take care of their own morale. No one is taking care of my morale."

9. *Mutual respect.* In not-so-great startup cultures, the business guys think the technical folks are more interested in cool technology than in building what the market wants. The technical side of the house thinks the business side isn't smart enough (or technical enough) to understand what the market wants. The architects look down on the developers who look down on QA. The sales team thinks marketing isn't doing its job in generating leads. Everyone thinks the sales team is overpaid and should be selling more. In great startup cultures, everyone shares a mutual respect for what each party brings to the

table and celebrates wins from wherever they come. Heated but healthy debate leads to decisions that are accepted, even if not everybody agrees with them.

10. *Customer-obsessed.* Great startup cultures are maniacally focused on defining who the customer is, what the customer wants and needs, and what the customer will value enough to pay for now. It starts well before a single line of code is written. These cultures value talking to as many potential customers as possible before a product is conceived. They make customer feedback a key part of the process once the product or service is delivered. Great startup cultures are rarely surprised by customer issues because they are proactive and process-oriented about understanding everything they can about their customers.

11. *High energy level.* You can literally feel it when you walk into a great startup culture. The room has energy. There's a buzz. Doors are open. Whiteboards are filled with hieroglyphics. People are getting stuff done. Meetings are short and to the point. You might trip over a dog.

12. *Fun.* Startups should be fun. In great startup cultures, everyone reinforces that fun is happening, even if it isn't at that particular time. Employees tell their friends how much fun they are having. Whining is unwelcome.

13. *Integrity.* Great startup cultures do not cut corners. They maintain the highest integrity in the way they treat customers, handle employee issues, write code, and go about their daily business. They have integrity when it is easy and, more importantly, when it is hard. This kind of integrity should not be confused with lacking toughness. Integrity in this sense means having a team with enough confidence in what it is building, and then delivering to customers, that cheating in any form or even just going halfway, is unacceptable.

Once you go beyond the founders and the first few employees, the culture of your new business will quickly start to develop. Most of the mentors in TechStars have been involved in starting more than one company and every one of them will tell you that there were many things they learned about creating a startup culture from mistakes they made, things they ignored, or issues they overlooked in their first business. While Greg's baker's dozen of the characteristics of a great startup culture may not be exactly right for you, coming up with your own list, being explicit about what matters with every person who joins your team, and continuing to live by the characteristics will go a long way toward helping you create a great company.

Greg's article originally appeared in techflash.com.

Two Strikes and You Are Out

Brad Feld

Brad is a managing director at Foundry Group and one of the co-founders of TechStars.

I live my life by a simple rule that I call the "Screw Me Once" rule. I permit everyone I work with to screw me over once. When this happens, I confront them, forgive them, and move on. However, if they screw me over a second time, then I'm done with them forever.

While the definition of *screw me* is vague, I put it in the category of deceitful or immoral behavior. The phrase "screw me" is deliberately aggressive and hostile in this context; behavior that qualifies is also deliberately aggressive and hostile.

I don't consider someone letting me down, not following through on a commitment, or failing at something to fall into this category. Failure is a fundamental part of entrepreneurship and I embrace it as part of the process. I fail often and I expect people whom I work with to fail also—either dramatically, or in lesser ways such as not following through on commitments.

Systemic behavior that doesn't correct, such as an inability to get closure on things, or a regular mismatch between the expectations that one sets and what one delivers, becomes a problem, but is not in the Screw Me category. Instead, this will decrease my desire to work with the person, lower my expectations about what will be accomplished, and make me cautious about my own engagement with them. But it won't cause me to be done with them.

If you lie to me, deceive me, purposefully hurt me (or someone I care about), do something I consider immoral, or do something

Brad Feld watches the shock and awe that follows an F-bomb.

that is illegal, that's one strike. However, I view addressing this as my responsibility because many people don't realize they've done this, or don't realize the potential impact and implications of their behavior. I try to be emotionally clear in my reaction—dispassionate, but not passive; direct, but not hostile; specific, yet not accusatory.

Occasionally, this approach simply doesn't work. In these cases, I just disengage and assume I'm not going to be able to develop a substantive relationship with that person. In my experience, however, a deep and thoughtful conversation usually ensues, which also serves to build a much stronger relationship or at least the potential for one.

Once the confrontation is resolved, I'm in a happy place again and don't ever think twice about whatever issue caused it. However, like a yellow card in soccer, you only get to trigger the Screw Me rule once. If it happens again, we're done. Forever.

I've handed out plenty of yellow cards and received a few. In a number of cases, my strongest relationships are with people who have gotten yellow cards. Fortunately, the list of people who have gotten the equivalent of a red card from me is very short.

Karma Matters

Warren Katz

Warren was the co-founder of MÄK Technologies, a company that makes distribution simulation software, and is now CEO of VT MÄK. He has been a TechStars mentor since 2009.

Photo Courtesy of MAK Technologies

As one goes through life, you wind up hanging out with family (mostly no choice), lovers (surprisingly little choice as well), friends (a lot of choice here), and business acquaintances (less choice). You also have a spectrum of things you do to live (work, earn money, pay bills) and things you live to do (wild sex, fixing cars, fishing, restoration of architectural millwork). The very luckiest among us get to hang out with the people we really like (whether by birth or choice), and do the things we really love (retire early, have a lifestyle job, have a hobby that pays the bills, or enjoy a perfectly directed career). Most people live on a spectrum of this—forced to do things they don't like and spend time with people they're not thrilled with in order to subsidize their preferred pursuits.

Business and making money are usually, and unfortunately, necessary evils that tend to push people toward spending more time with those they don't like and doing things they don't want to do so they can maximize the freedom that more money can provide. Also, in business, when one person gives something to another that results in an increase in remuneration (a raise, an introduction to a new customer, a recommendation), there is inevitably the sense of debt or payment owed for such favor. This is one of the main differences between business relationships and personal relationships; the accrual of indebtedness and how they are viewed.

In my personal relationships, I enjoy the feeling of freely doing favors for friends and family that endear me to them and make them happy. I also enjoy the feeling of someone else freely doing me a favor because they really like me and want me to be happy. I prefer being in a surplus situation, where I have done more for my loved ones than they have done for me. This would be the exact opposite in business, where one might feel cheated or used if there were a negative balance of trade.

So it's a rare occasion when one finds oneself in a business relationship that has the characteristics of a friendship (or a friendship that starts making money). Such is the case with one of my closest friends, Brad Feld (otherwise known as Vladimir Schlockfeld to those who know his true identity.)

My wife Ilana worked for Brad at his first company, Feld Technologies. Though Brad and I never worked together, we certainly felt the kinship of fellow entrepreneurs. Brad was a couple of years ahead of me in the pursuit of our mutual startups. I considered Brad a mentor and not coincidentally the very first dollar of business that MĀK Technologies billed was to Brad's company to do some system administration work for one of Feld Technologies' clients. He could have obtained those services elsewhere for less money, but I knew he was doing it just to do me a favor and help get my company off the ground. And so it began.

A few years later, Brad showed up at my house with a demo of a music-generating game product with which a user could manipulate a joystick and generate reasonable sounding music. A couple of brilliant guys out of the MIT Media Lab came up with this technology and Brad was going to be their first outside investor. It was a relatively tiny amount of money by today's standards and I'm guessing that Brad felt that it would make him look better in the eyes of the Media Lab guys if he could persuade a couple of his other entrepreneur buddies to co-invest. Remembering that first dollar of revenue at MĀK, I would have invested in anything Brad asked me to (and that still is pretty much the case to this day). So, I wrote the biggest investment check of my life (until that day) and with the peace of mind felt by someone giving a charitable donation jumped into the boat with Brad (and the two MIT geniuses).

Over the course of the next decade-plus, every once in a while Brad and I would call each other to tell the other about something we were throwing some money into and ask if the other was interested, much the same way I might ask another friend to go fishing with me, my wife to go out to dinner, or my brother or sister to go in on an anniversary gift for our parents. When I receive such calls, I answer them with the mindset: "My friend is calling me to go out and play." As Brad and his wife, Amy, my wife, Ilana, and I often vacation together, the topics are often commingled anyway. Even though many of the investments went belly-up, we were in it together and having fun.

Brad recently e-mailed me because he and his partner Jason Mendelson at Foundry Group were thinking about investing in a motion capture company in New York City called Organic Motion. I'm in the simulation industry, so I'm a consumer of motion capture technology and know some of the players. I also know some people in the video game industry, so I can reach out and find out what the scoop is on these guys. I was a little puzzled at first since the motion capture market is pretty crowded and the consumers are mostly video game companies that are notoriously cheap and have huge "not invented here" syndrome. I was wondering why my friend was considering throwing money at something like that. But, Brad had asked me to check it out, so I had one conference call with the company, and lo and behold, they appeared to have something that nobody else had. I hopped in my car a couple of weeks later to visit them and I was completely blown away by what they had created. So here we have an example of a favor that I think I'm doing for Brad that turns out to be one he is actually doing for me. Jason and Brad allowed me to throw in some money alongside the Foundry Group investment and away we went.

When I look back on the last 20 years, I actually don't have any other relationship like this other than with my wife, who theoretically owns half my stuff. Having a deep friendship combined with a hobby that actually makes money is pretty cool (hobby for me, profession for him). Not too common. You hear about other famous relationships like this (Buffett and Munger, Gates and Allen) and perhaps it's a little unfair to crow too loudly about this because we're very much in the black together on our investments, but I would flatter myself to think that even if we were losing overall the relationship would still have that friendship, camaraderie, and trust at its core.

Oh, by the way, that favor I did Brad by throwing money into that strange music game company to help him look good in front of the Media Lab guys? That little investment I tried to write off as a tax loss to offset gains from the sale of MÄK? That company, Harmonix, came out with a game a decade after our initial investment called Guitar Hero, and then another called Rock Band, before being acquired by Viacom for $325 million, making my tiny investment worth a lot. Karma.

You'll read more about this in a later chapter by Eran Egozy titled "Practice Your Passion." Recently Warren, Brad, and Eran had dinner together in Cambridge and reflected on the various things they had worked together on over the years. As MIT graduates, they talked about how they were helping the newest generation of MIT entrepreneurs. They also sat quietly and appreciated each other's friendship independent of any particular business or financial success. It was a great evening.

Karma is the tie that binds all of the TechStars mentors. We are often asked "What do they get out of it?" Sure—there's the fame and glory (ha!) and the chance to invest in the companies. But aside from a nice annual dinner, our mentors aren't compensated. We think most of the mentors will tell you they're in it for the karma. They simply love helping energetic entrepreneurs, and they assume something good will come out of it some day. We think most of them will tell you that something good already has.

Be Open to Randomness

David Cohen

David is a co-founder and the CEO of TechStars.

Take a moment and think back to all the good things that have happened to you so far in your life. If you're like me and you contemplate that list, you'll realize that many of those good things came about in very random ways. Perhaps it's the way that you met your significant other, or how you decided on the college you'd go to. Maybe it's how you got that great job offer, or how you found out that your favorite band was playing down the street on your last business trip.

I think it's important to be open to randomness in your life. Many of the most successful people I know are very deliberate about randomness. Brad Feld is a great example. For many years, Brad has regularly held "random days" when he'll meet anyone to talk about anything for 15 minutes. He does this back to back for an entire day once in a while. Brad has no expectation about meetings on his random day. They're meetings that he normally wouldn't take or at least that he has no specific reason to take. But he figures he'll meet a few interesting people, and maybe something good will come out of it once in a while.

Now, guess how I met Brad Feld. It was on one of his random days. And on that random day, guess what we talked about? TechStars! I had never met Brad but I had been a fan and reader of his blog. I had no expectation that Brad would actually take an interest in TechStars. I certainly had no expectation that he'd help me co-found it and be an amazing partner. During this 10-minute meeting, Brad expressed his interest in investing. Unheard of! This was as random as it gets. And it led directly to TechStars being what it is today.

Today, I too have the random day tradition. I've met some really interesting people, made new friends, and even found some investments this way.

On one of my random days, I met a local entrepreneur named Sean Porter. Sean was building a company called Gigbot, and would just come by occasionally and ask for some advice. Gigbot would later be acquired by TicketFly, and Sean graciously granted me advisor options just before the acquisition. Through this randomness, I'm now a small shareholder in TicketFly, which is a company that I'm very excited about. Another example of someone that I met randomly is Rob La Gesse, who is the chief disruption officer at Rackspace. They've since become an amazing supporter of Tech-Stars and have sponsored The Founders, which is a video series that we do every year. Through Rob, I met Robert Scoble, who now attends TechStars demo events and has also become a fan of the program.

Being open to randomness is about more than just taking meetings with people. It's the idea of trying something you really have no reason to try. Recognize the fact that someone you meet or something that you do might ultimately be able to help you in some completely unexpected way. If you're not open to randomness, you may miss a huge opportunity to advance your company, find a customer, a business partner, or maybe even a lifelong friend. How random is that?

David Cohen and Brad Feld randomly eating and drinking at Red Rocks Amphitheater during an outing with the TechStars of 2009 to watch *Office Space*.

THEME 3: EXECUTION

It's often said that startups are controlled chaos. There are so many things going on and so much to do. The best entrepreneurs are those who can manage the chaos, focus on what's important, and find a way to execute efficiently.

Efficiency of execution is so important to startups that we have deliberately designed processes to detect it as part of the TechStars application process. We look for concise and direct e-mails instead of endless phone calls. We're more impressed by founders who supplement their applications with quick and dirty videos that show the basics of what they're doing than with those who waste time on production value. While we can't give all of our application processing secrets away, there are dozens of other clues that help us determine if the team has one of the most important entrepreneurial traits—the ability to get stuff done and focus on results.

Some entrepreneurs, like Jeff Powers and Vikas Reddy of Occipital, are execution machines. You know that whenever they put their mind to something they'll grind it out and get it done. Others, like Andy Smith of DailyBurn, sneak up on you with their calm, quiet competence. Before you know it, they've created something beautiful and amazing that appeals to numerous people. Then there are entrepreneurs like Ari Newman and Tom Chikoore of Filtrbox, who study their data obsessively but can turn on a dime when they see that the path they are going down isn't working.

Execution doesn't mean blindly going from point A to point B without collecting an enormous amount of data from many different sources along the way. Great entrepreneurs know how to synthesize these data, make a decision about the path they are going down, and execute.

Do More Faster

David Cohen

David is a co-founder and the CEO of TechStars.

Startups do almost everything at a disadvantage. Initially, most startups have less money than their competitors. Startups have less credibility. They have fewer customers. They have fewer employees, which means there are typically fewer people focused on things like marketing, sales, and product development. Resources are scarce at a startup.

But, just like in the martial arts, the best startups use the weight of their opponents against them. Bureaucracy slows down larger companies. People do less because making a mistake can be politically costly. Risk takers who are wrong get fired or lose power internally. The larger the company, the more likely it is to be slow.

If there's one competitive advantage that most startups have, it's that they can do more faster. And because they can do more faster they can learn more faster. They can immediately throw things away that don't work because nobody cares anyway. Nobody is trying to protect a brand that doesn't exist, and nobody has any reason to be afraid of small failures. Startups know that's just part of the process.

When you ask CEOs of major companies what they're most worried about, one common answer is "a couple of guys in a garage somewhere." Why? Because their larger and more established competitors have too much to lose to try something radically different. There's too much at stake for these large companies to try to blow up the market to disrupt the existing players. Relatively speaking, startups have nothing to lose and everything to gain by trying radical or non-obvious things. Larger companies are often baffled at just how much a startup can get done and it scares them.

One of the things we talk about with our startups at TechStars is that they simply have to do more faster. This doesn't mean doing random stuff—they still have to be thoughtful. But if they're not hyperproductive as small, nimble companies, then they're fighting from a real disadvantage. I'm such a big believer in this that I named my own angel fund Bullet Time Ventures. It's named after the move from the movie *The Matrix*, in which Neo is so fast that he can easily dodge bullets. His enemies seem so slow and he has an obvious advantage over them that can make all the difference in the (in his case, virtual) world.

When Occipital was in TechStars in 2008, they were faster than a speeding bullet. As a visual search company, they tried several products before having a runaway hit with RedLaser. All of them were interesting, but what really paid off for Occipital was their ability to try their ideas quickly and throw away what didn't work while focusing on what did. RedLaser was the fourth product Occipital worked on in about six months. This may sound disorganized and random on the surface, but Jeff and Vikas were very deliberate about assessing progress at every step.

Next Big Sound built an incredibly beautiful and functional product in under three months. SendGrid figured out how to scale their e-mail delivery infrastructure to 20 million e-mails a day in under a year. Oneforty rallied a community of thousands of Twitter application developers in just a few months. Intense Debate went from concept to being installed on hundreds of blogs in the course of a single summer. Companies that work just always seem to move at lightning pace. By contrast, the ones that don't seem to always be talking about releases and features that are coming "in a few months."

How do the fast companies do it? They focus on what matters, and make massive progress in the areas that actually have an impact.

At TechStars and as an angel investor in general, I've been involved with a few startups that couldn't do more faster. They were just as slow to execute as larger competitors. They employed too much process too early, tried to convince themselves that they were absolutely right before taking risks, and thought at the expense of doing. Their great ideas couldn't save them. It turns out that giving up your one obvious competitive advantage often proves to be deadly. If a startup can't do more faster, it usually just gets dead faster.

The view leaving David Cohen's office at the TechStars "Bunker." The founders will often jump up to slap the phrase on the way out after a meeting.

Assume that You're Wrong

Howard Diamond

Howard is the CEO and chairman of ThinIdentity Corporation, a health care identity company, and has previously served as CEO and chairman of both Corporate Software and ePartners. He has been a TechStars mentor since 2007.

Learning how to say, "I was wrong" is one of the hardest things to teach an entrepreneur. This is a real problem since most of us are often wrong despite inclinations to the contrary.

When starting or running a business, making mistakes is a given. It is often obvious that a bad decision was made and it's usually easy to correct. However, before you can correct a bad decision, you have to admit you made a bad decision; for most people that is the difficult part. As a result, it is critical to create an environment in every business in which everyone throughout the organization is comfortable admitting mistakes. For this to be effective, it has to be driven from the top.

I was a co-founder of a startup in 1990 called Course Technology. In five years, we were able to build into a successful business, with $75 million in sales and 20 percent net income. We sold the company to a large publishing group (then called ITP) and were even able to overachieve on the earn-out that was a part of the deal. That sounds great and it was.

The things that drove most of our success as we built the company were only vaguely connected to the original business plan. As a management team, we needed to constantly revise our strategy and our market approach based on what we learned. We had to be willing to let go of our own assumptions and really listen to what we were hearing from our customers and our partners. We had to listen when employees had concerns with things that senior management initially saw as givens. The sales model and pricing structures that drove the company's success changed dramatically from their initial designs. We had to go to our board and tell our investors that what we had told them earlier had turned out to be incorrect, but that we were able to make changes as we went along that adjusted our course and still allowed us to exceed expectations.

One of the things that has been so exhilarating about being a part of TechStars is to see the amazing changes that so many of the companies go through during their participation in the program. Often, the teams that are the most exciting at Demo Day are the ones that have traveled the furthest from what they thought about their businesses when they applied to the program. There is an enormous difference between exciting technology and an exciting business. Understanding those differences and being able to make changes as they are needed is often the difference between success and failure.

In 2009, at the first TechStars "Meet the Mentors" event, the team that I enjoyed meeting with the most was Next Big Sound. Their business plan, however, didn't make sense to me. As they talked to other mentors that evening, it was clear that a number of us had the same reaction. Everyone thought they were great guys with a business plan that didn't inspire much support or enthusiasm from any of us.

As I sat in the audience at TechStars Boulder Demo Day at the end of the summer, I watched the same team knock it out of the park. I was immensely proud of these guys, not just because I believed that they now had a business, but because they had really listened to, understood, and incorporated many of the thoughts and ideas they heard from their mentors over the summer. As a result, they created a business that was exciting, fundable, and had real potential.

Howard epitomizes the entrepreneur who has massive conviction about what he is doing but is willing to quickly admit when he is wrong. As an executive, Howard takes a clear position and goes after it. When it doesn't work, he acknowledges the situation, synthesizes the data, and tries a different course of action. He leads his team from the front—being willing to break new ground but also take the blame when things don't work out.

He really shines as a mentor and a board member. He challenges entrepreneurs to have a point of view. If they don't, or their point of view is weak, he increases the pressure. He doesn't feel the need to discover the answer at the beginning, but he does believe everyone should have a clear hypothesis and go after it with conviction.

In this way, he is completely comfortable being wrong. It's not a fault; rather it's stimuli to get to the correct answer faster. If you assume that you are wrong, you will ultimately find the right answer faster and be very confident and satisfied when you do.

Howard Diamond (left of center) shares his experience with incoming founders at Meet the Mentors night during the summer of 2009.

Make Decisions Quickly

Ari Newman

Ari is the CEO and co-founder of Filtrbox, a web service that tracks and monitors new media content and news for small- to medium-size businesses as well as individuals. Filtrbox raised about $1 million from True Ventures and Flywheel Ventures after completing TechStars in 2007. It was acquired by Jive Software in 2010.

Filtrbox lives in a real-time world, both in terms of what we do and how we operate the business. The ability to collect data, look at the facts, and make decisions quickly is a huge asset to an early stage company. In the words of the great hockey player Wayne Gretzky, you have to "skate to where the puck is going."

One of the most valuable assets an early stage company has is that it is nimble. The number of constraints on the business is very limited compared to years down the road when you have a complex product, revenue streams, and masses of customers. The consequence of not making decisions quickly is akin to giving up one of your best assets.

At Filtrbox we started the company with the vision of solving the "information overload" problem for business professionals. We launched with a *freemium* model, through which we gave away a limited version of our software for free and—if you liked it and wanted more—you could pay for the full version. We lived the mantra of "build something valuable, get the word out, and listen to your customers. Then iterate and repeat."

We also paid close attention to what our metrics told us since we could track everything our users did. It didn't take long to see that people loved Filtrbox, but we had to pick up the phone and talk to people to demonstrate the full value and get them to part with dollars to pay for the full version. We looked at everything, things like number of customer interactions, average deal size, and time to close. We could have spent months trying to fine-tune the signup process, the in-trial call to action, or the onboarding process. We knew Filtrbox was delivering the best value to brands, brand managers, and those who needed to listen to their customers.

So, instead of continuing to endlessly collect new data, we looked at where the market was going, where we thought the real-time Web would deliver value, where our core customers were coming from, and how they were finding us. Once we started thinking this way, the answer became very clear. We chose to skate to where the puck was going and leverage our greatest assets—our nimbleness and the software platform we had created. In May 2009, we changed gears and decided to focus squarely on the real-time social media monitoring space.

Today we are seeing excellent growth and are using our assets to our advantage. We continue to operate in the same way, collecting data, looking at metrics, and making quick decisions. Changes come daily, weekly, and monthly—not once a quarter or once a year. Since we have an inside sales model, we get to talk to customers and prospects all day, every day. As a result, we are continually learning what our customers want and we are able to quickly make decisions and change directions to meet their needs. I hope to hold on to this style for as long as we can at Filtrbox.

In January 2010, Jive Software acquired Filtrbox. Ari had been running around raising new financing when he ran into a couple of companies in the enterprise social computing market that were very interested in incorporating social data from the real-time Web into their products. Both Jive and Filtrbox shared similar technology platforms and visions of how this could work, and Jive had established itself as one of the market leaders in enterprise social computing. We watched as Ari evaluated his options thoughtfully and then decided to join forces with Jive.

Six months later, the acquisition looks like it is working out great. The Filtrbox team in Boulder is expanding quickly and has been fully integrated into Jive, which has offices in Silicon Valley and Portland. Filtrbox's product has been rebranded as the Jive social media monitoring solution and all indications are that it's being well received by many new customers.

It's Just Data

Bill Warner

Bill is the founder of Avid Technology (the pioneer in video editing software) and Wildfire Communications. He is also a co-founder of TechStars in Boston.

Good advice is a good thing, right? Therefore, lots of good advice should be an even better thing.

Well, not really. But we do it anyway at TechStars as the companies get flooded with good advice and some bad advice, too. I know, since I have provided both kinds to them.

In the TechStars Boston 2009 program, two brothers Monaghan, Mike and Tom, started a company called TempMine. The initial idea was simple: build a marketplace for temporary workers through which they can market themselves, let them sell themselves directly to hiring companies, and cut out the middleman. Tom and Mike's premise was that eliminating the agencies would be a good thing.

The summer began with advice from many fronts, including negative ones suggesting TempMine would be breaking the law, labor rules are strict and impossible to work around, and there's no way someone can work directly for companies on a 1099 wage-reporting tax form. So Mike and Tom started reworking the plan.

At the same time, I spent time talking with Tom about what really drove him to start the company in the first place. He realized that he was motivated to help people find the right job direction and he thought temping was one way to do that. This was useful, but then I started to push him on why he was focused only on temping. Why not help people find the right direction in their career, however it takes shape? Tom got excited about this and began exploring changing the name of the company to GlideHire to expand its perspective beyond temping.

At first this seemed exciting, but after a while, Tom came back and said, "Hey, it really is about temps—this is the thing I think will help the people I want as customers to find the right direction. I'm going back to the TempMine name and the earlier plan." For a little while, I felt bad that I had helped clarify things on the one hand while helping fuel a tangent on the other. While it was only a detour of a week, that's a lot in TechStars time.

But then I realized that this is part of how TechStars works. The companies get connected with mentors who care and who provide input. The input is diverse and it will be conflicting. Even input from a trusted advisor will have elements that are just not right. The founders are quickly forced to realize that they cannot create a solution that incorporates all of the inputs they are getting. Their only hope instead is to listen to their head and their heart and follow a path that they believe in, keeping some of the feedback and discarding other thoughts and ideas.

So, is too much conflicting advice a bad thing? Nope. Having too much advice can teach you how to make better decisions, as long as you accept that conflicting information is a part of life. Remember that it's just data.

Saying "It's just data" is one of the most common ways to end a mentor meeting at TechStars. We try hard to help mentors be as effective as possible, and one of the things that strong mentors, especially ones who are entrepreneurs, have to be careful of is not being too forceful with their advice. Experienced entrepreneurs usually believe they know the right answer and, while they often do, part of the magic of TechStars is to help the TechStars founders discover the right answer. And, as any successful entrepreneur knows, there are often multiple correct answers. So, as a mentor, being clear that you are only providing data and that it is ultimately up to the entrepreneur to make the decision is an important way to approach giving advice.

Use Your Head, then Trust Your Gut

Ryan McIntyre

Ryan was a co-founder of Excite.com and is currently a managing director at Foundry Group.

You can't manage what you don't measure. The importance of instrumenting your business properly to enable intelligent decision making cannot be overstated. This is particularly true for companies that run their businesses on the Web. A mountain of otherwise unavailable quantitative data is there for the taking. Every single user interaction can be measured and those data can be tremendously valuable when properly interpreted.

On the other hand, starting a company and creating a product that didn't previously exist in a market segment that may not have previously existed is a murky proposition at best. And there are often precious little data to go on in the earliest days of a company's life. And when available, the data are often confusing. Furthermore, a company's friends, mentors, advisors, and board members often give conflicting advice. Market research and user focus groups can yield inconsistent data and lead to conclusions that are in opposition to one another.

What is an early stage founder to do? Let me offer two bits of conflicting advice (get used to that!). First, be suspicious of your data. Consider everything that you hear, measure, and learn to be anecdotal even if it is corroborated by several sources. Second, especially early on, remember to gather as much data as possible and measure every aspect of your business. If you don't instill this discipline at the beginning, you'll never catch up, and you'll never have the right information to make the right decisions.

Be prepared for the data to give you a head fake. Early success with a certain customer segment might lead to a decision to focus on a subgroup of customers that turns out to be really hard to sell to and which happens to represent only 4 percent of the overall customer base. Don't be like the guy looking for his lost car keys late at night in the parking lot who is looking only underneath the lamppost because that is the only place he can see. Constantly revisit the data—measuring the wrong things can be worse than measuring nothing. For example, if you are running an ad-supported media site, a maniacal focus on increasing page views per user session might frustrate loyal users and could drastically reduce ad click-through rates and ultimately harm the business.

Remember to think exponentially, especially in the world of technology. A few early data points on a geometric curve might lead you to conclude that you're observing a linear phenomenon, which would lead to some seriously erroneous predictions about what points farther up the curve might look like. To paraphrase Ray Kurzweil, when presented with exponential growth, remember that people tend to drastically overestimate what will happen in the short term, but will profoundly underestimate what happens over longer time spans.

It has been said that one measure of intelligence is the ability to hold contradictory thoughts in one's mind simultaneously. Well, consider life as a founder of a startup to be one big intelligence test. In the end, you'll need to get comfortable living with messy and incomplete data. Remember that living the startup life requires both art and science and is simultaneously qualitative and quantitative. Take all the inputs you can gather and then make the decisions that feel right to both your head and your gut.

Ryan McIntyre offers potentially conflicting advice at TechStars in 2009.

Progress Equals Validated Learning

Eric Ries

Eric is the co-founder and CTO of IMVU and is the author of The Lean Startup Methodology.

Would you rather have $30,000 or $1,000,000 in revenues for your startup? Sounds like a no-brainer, but I'd like to try and convince you that it's not.

This may sound crazy, coming as it does from an advocate of charging customers for your product from Day One. I have counseled innumerable entrepreneurs to change their focus to revenue, and many companies that refuse this advice get themselves into trouble by running out of time. Yet revenue alone is not a sufficient goal. Focusing on it exclusively can lead to failure as surely as ignoring it altogether.

Consider a company that has a million dollars of revenue and is showing growth quarter after quarter. Yet their investors are frustrated. Every board meeting, the metrics of success change. Their product definition fluctuates wildly—one month, it's a dessert top-ping; the next, it's a floor wax. Their product development team is hard at work on a next-generation product platform, which is de-signed to offer a new suite of products—but this effort is way behind schedule. In fact, this company hasn't shipped any new products in months. And yet their numbers continue to grow, month after month. What's going on?

The diagnosis is easy: The entrepreneurs are exceptionally gifted salesmen. This is an incredible skill, one that most engineers over-look. True salesmen are artists, able to hone in on just those key words, phrases, features, and benefits that will persuade another hu-man being to give up their hard-earned money in exchange for even an early product. For a startup, having great sales DNA is a wonderful asset. But at the early stages, it can devour the company's future.

The problem stems from selling each customer a customized one-time product. This is the magic of sales: By learning about each customer in depth, the amazing salesman can convince each of them that this product would solve serious problems. That leads to cashing plenty of checks. Now, in some situations, this overselling would lead to a secondary problem, namely, that customers would realize they had been duped and refuse to keep being customers. But here's where a truly great sales artist comes in. Customers don't usually mind a bait-and-switch if the switched-to product really does solve an important problem for them. These salesmen used their insight into what their customers really needed to make the sale and then deliver something of even greater value. They are closing orders. They are gaining valuable customer data. They are close to breakeven. What's the problem?

This approach is fundamentally nonscalable. Every sale requires handholding and personal attention from the founders themselves. This process cannot be delegated because it's impossible to explain to a normal person what's involved in making the sale. The founders have a lethal combination of insight about what potential customers want and in-depth knowledge about what their current product can really deliver. As a result, potential customers are being turned away; they can only afford to engage with the customers who are best qualified.

Let me describe a different company, one with only $30,000 in revenue. This company has a large long-term vision, but their current product is only a fraction of what they hope to build. Compared to the million-dollar startup, they are operating at a micro scale. How does that stack up?

First of all, they are not selling their product by hand. Instead, each potential customer has to go through a self-serve process of signing up and paying money. Because they have no presence in the market, they have to find distribution channels to bring in customers. They can only afford channels such as Google that support buying in small volume.

Compensating for these limitations is that they know each of their customers extremely well and they are constantly experimenting with new product features and product marketing to increase the yield on each new crop of customers they bring in. They have found, over time, a formula for acquiring, qualifying, and selling customers in the market segments they have targeted. Most importantly, they have lots of data about the unit economics of their business. They know how much it costs to bring in a customer and they know how much money they can expect to make on each one.

In other words, they have learned to grow renewable audiences. Given the data they've collected about these early customers, they are also able to estimate with modest precision how big the market is for their product in its current form. They may be at micro-scale now, but they are in a very good position to raise venture money and engage in extremely rapid growth.

Our million-dollar startup, by contrast, is stuck in the mud.

Stories like these have led me to this definition of progress for a startup: *validated learning about customers*. This unit of progress is remarkable. First of all, it means that most aggregate measures of success, like total revenue, are not very useful. They don't tell us the key things we need to know about the business: how profitable is it on a per-customer basis? What's the total available market? What's the return on investment on acquiring new customers? How do existing customers respond to our product over time?

Validated learning about customers locates progress firmly in the heads of the people inside the company and not in any artifacts the company produces. That's why none of the dollars, milestones, products, or code can count as progress. Given a choice between what a successful team has learned and the source code they have produced, I would take validated learning every time.

While the phrase "progress equals validated learning" might seem chewy and theoretical, it's actually a brilliant combination of words. Fundamentally, all startups want to make progress. But as Eric points out, the measures of progress are often wrong and misleading, especially at the early stages. Using the filter of "validated learning" (namely—something that you've learned that you know is true) is a powerful frame of reference that forces more discipline into the discussion.

We've gotten to know Eric well over the past few years and think his work on the Lean Startup Methodology is incredible. We encourage all entrepreneurs to become disciples of Eric.

The Plural of Anecdote Is Not Data

Brad Feld

Brad is a managing director at Foundry Group and one of the co-founders of TechStars.

A phrase that is often heard around TechStars is "the plural of anecdote is not data." While the original attribution of this quote is murky (see http://bit.ly/anecdt) the meaning is powerful and applies importantly to both mentors and entrepreneurs.

Many of the mentors in TechStars are experienced entrepreneurs. They often have started multiple companies—some successful, some not—and have a wide range of experiences. Through this experience, they've developed many stories and built anecdotes from them. These anecdotes are endearing, funny, clever, powerful, and repeated often, but they need to be put in their proper place in the information hierarchy.

While there is much for entrepreneurs to learn from storytelling and anecdotes, they run the risk of generalizing anecdotes into truths. During TechStars, entrepreneurs often get conflicting stories and advice from mentors. Mentor A believes that you should go after a specific vertical market as your market entry strategy and then explains how this worked for him in his first company. Mentor B, in a separate conversation, explains how a specific vertical market approach failed her in her first company and was a key contributor to its demise. Instead, she suggests starting out with a broadly horizontal platform approach, being careful to start picking off specific vertical markets as the customers start to emerge in bulk from them. In each case, they tell nice anecdotes that support their perspective.

What should the entrepreneur do? We start by saying, "It's only data," meaning that the entrepreneur needs to synthesize the data—especially different perspectives—and form his own opinion about the correct course of action. If you take an additional step back from the problem, however, you realize that a single anecdote isn't enough to generate usable data from.

One of our goals at TechStars is to surround first-time entrepreneurs with mentors who can flood them with stories, anecdotes, advice, and data. We view it as a huge advantage when there are enough of these, and they conflict, because they then force the entrepreneur to go deeper, think harder about what is going on, and

TechStars mentor Howard Lindzon delivers anecdotal evidence during TechStars in the summer of 2008.

apply it to his specific situation. If he only relied on one anecdote to form a point of view, he'd miss the variety of different circumstances that could affect him and his company.

It's often said that the information hierarchy starts with data, builds to information, and eventually peaks with knowledge. Yet, in the entrepreneurial world, I've found that anecdotes come even before data, and it's important to have a broad number of them before you start abstracting up to the data layer. Hence the phrase "The plural of anecdote is not data."

Don't Suck at E-Mail

David Cohen

David is a co-founder and the CEO of TechStars.

During orientation each year, we implore the founders who are going through TechStars not to suck at e-mail. Sucking at e-mail is a surefire way to get your mentors, potential investors, and customers to lose interest in you.

There are many ways that new founders can suck at e-mail, but there are a few common ones that can be corrected quickly. First, change your attitude. The most common excuse, "I get too much e-mail," is ridiculous. We all get a ton of e-mail. I explain to the founders during orientation that it's extremely unlikely that they get as much e-mail as I do. Reject and remove this excuse from your vocabulary because e-mail volume is no reason to suck at e-mail. In fact, entrepreneurs should want even more e-mail, especially from your customers.

If you accept the notion that "you can't get too much e-mail," you'll then need a system for dealing with it. We recommend something similar to the Getting Things Done (GTD) system by David

Allen, which includes tactics such as "inbox zero." Your goal should be to touch every e-mail only once and either respond to it immediately or put it on a to-do list with a due date to be dealt with later. Then, delete the item from your inbox. Do not use your inbox as your to-do list—this is a guaranteed path to e-mail misery. This simple solution will keep most people from sucking at e-mail. If your inbox has 2,000 new messages in it right now, you probably suck at e-mail.

Use e-mail as a branding opportunity. Many entrepreneurs send e-mail from a generic gmail, yahoo, or hotmail address. This is silly—every time you send an e-mail like this you're missing a branding opportunity for your company. Send and receive e-mail from your company domain so that every time someone gets an e-mail from you they will think about your company.

Taking weeks to respond to e-mail or not responding at all are also terrific ways to suck at e-mail. As a general rule, you should try to delete or respond to e-mail within a day or two. If you are on vacation or out of pocket, set up an auto-responder so that people know what's going on. If you don't know how to answer an e-mail, reply quickly and say that you're going to think about it (and set up a to-do item).

Perhaps the biggest way that people suck at e-mail is simply by not being concise and direct. Enough said.

Mark O'Sullivan of Vanilla came up with seven rules to not suck at e-mail. They are so good that we are repeating his blog post about them here.

1. Use the subject line—Sounds simple, but it amazes me how many people send out e-mails with useless subjects like "hey," or worse—no subject at all. The subject line is not only the first glimpse a person gets of your reason for contacting them (which is extremely important if you are e-mailing someone cold), but it also is a key piece of information that people might search on when trying to find your e-mail some time down the road. Take a moment to actually think about the purpose of your e-mail. Keep it between two and seven words. Make it descriptive and succinct.

2. The "three sentence rule"—This is one that can be tricky to use across all e-mails you send, but it is definitely worth using when you are reaching out to people whom you don't know personally, you have never contacted before, or you know suck at replying to e-mails. Keep your e-mail body down to three sentences. I know that you might feel the need to put more information into an e-mail than three sentences, but the reality is that

the people on the other end of the line are giant question marks. You don't know how busy they are, how much they suck at e-mail, how interested they are in what you have to say, and so on. If you write more than three sentences, there is a high likelihood that they will not reply to your e-mail. It can be challenging at first, but you'll eventually find that you can get your point across in an extremely succinct manner. Ask only one question, and put it in your last sentence. This leaves the question lingering in the other person's mind, and it allows them to quickly shoot you back a response without feeling the pressure of a mass volume, heavy content e-mail that will require more than one minute of their time. Most importantly, it gets the volley of conversation started, so your more detailed questions or information can follow up in a conversation that the other person is now invested in.

3. Spell check—If you are not great at spelling, use the spell checker. Nothing makes you look worse than bad spelling and bad grammar. Simple, but true.

4. Reply to important e-mails right away—I used to get important e-mails and decide that I needed to think about the response for a long time before replying. I didn't want to send knee-jerk e-mails back that had incomplete information. So, I'd wait a day, maybe two days, or sometimes as long as a week. Two things happen when you do this: First, the person on the other end thinks that you didn't get the e-mail, you don't care about the e-mail, or you are a complete idiot. Second, you could possibly forget to ever reply at all. So, when I get important e-mails, I reply to them right away—even if I don't have all of the information the person needs. I'll tell the person that I don't have it, but I'll get it to them by a certain date, and then I set a reminder and make sure that I get them that information by the time I said I would.

5. Use "unread" status—This is a habit I've picked up, and I find it extremely useful. If I read an e-mail that isn't very important, but does require a response from me, I'll leave it marked as unread until I have the time or information required to respond. Every time I open my e-mail program, I see X unread messages, and I am reminded of the e-mails I need to respond to. At least once a day I know I have the time to respond to those e-mails (typically first thing in the morning), so I'll go back and make sure that everyone gets the information they need.

6. Be conscious of how much you suck—If you send out e-mails that you consider important and you don't get a response, think about why that might be. Go back to the preceding points and compare the rules to the e-mail you sent: Did you use a descriptive subject? Was the body of your e-mail full of too much information, or did you stick to the three-sentence rule? Did you ask only one question, or did you manage to squeeze more than one question into your three sentences? Did you have spelling mistakes? Was your grammar so bad that the e-mail didn't even make sense? If you've done a good job on all of those points, then we fall into point 4: the person you are trying to contact (a) didn't get the e-mail, (b) doesn't care about the e-mail, or (c) is a complete idiot. Because so many people suck at e-mail, I've often found myself falling into the (b) category. No matter which way the cookie crumbles, you need to remember the most important rule of all when sending e-mails. . . .

7. Be persistent—No matter what the reason is for someone not replying to you, persistence will get you everywhere. The best way to be persistent and not be annoying is to use Rules 1, 2, and 3. Keep your e-mails about the business at hand, and don't let emotion get involved—which can be difficult if you're dealing with someone who sucks at e-mail. The last bit of advice I can give on this point is to remember that we all live in the real world. E-mail is fast and easy, but the reality is that not everyone uses it, and not everyone cares about it. I know it's scary, but if you're dealing with someone who sucks at e-mail, sometimes you just have to pick up the phone and call.

David Cohen aiming for "inbox zero" on a summer Saturday at The Bunker.

Use What's Free

Ben Huh

Ben is the CEO of The Cheezburger Network, owner of popular sites such as Lolcats, Loldogs, and FAIL Blog, and has made more people laugh than anyone we know. He's been a TechStars mentor since 2009.

One way to get leverage over all of the big players out there that you're competing with is to build your business to be more efficient than theirs. This is really easy for me because I'm a cheap bastard.

The Cheezburger Network serves over 10 million page views every day. Luckily for me, I have no idea how many servers it takes to do that. The reason is because we use WordPress (free!) to host our content. We also use YouTube (free!) to host our videos. We share information in the company using Google Apps (free!) and every day I jump on Skype to talk (free!) and videoconference (free!) with people around the world. We use dozens of open source applications (free!) to run our business. Our philosophy is to outsource everything that we're not great at to someone who is a proven and scalable leader, preferably without paying them.

Because we have this philosophy, our developers get to spend 90 percent of their time doing something valuable instead of chasing down complexity. We don't have anybody doing any kind of IT support, because that's not our job. Remember that human nature has a tendency to admire complexity, but to reward simplicity. Complexity has an inverse effect on the ability to scale your business. The more complicated you make your business, the harder it is to expand it. So stick with proven solutions and keep it simple. You may have to give up a few features here and there, but you'll be more nimble as a company.

By using what's free and avoiding complexity, you'll find that you can do more faster.

Every great startup entrepreneur uses the tools Ben mentions and more. In addition to WordPress, YouTube, Google Apps, and Skype, the TechStars companies told us that they routinely use the following free or very inexpensive products:

- Balsamiq for screen prototyping
- DimDim for web meetings
- DropBox for file storage and sharing
- Evernote for organizing tidbits of information
- Gist for keeping on top of your contacts
- GitHub for source code sharing
- Jing for screencasting
- MogoTest (TechStars 2009) for making sure your applications look great on every browser
- Pivotal Tracker for issue tracking
- SendGrid (TechStars 2009) for e-mail delivery
- SnapABug (TechStars 2009) for chatting with customers who visit your web site
- Twilio for audio conferencing and phone and SMS services
- Vanilla (TechStars 2009) for hosting a great forum for your community

Be Tiny Until You Shouldn't Be

Jeffrey Powers

Jeffrey is a co-founder of Occipital, which uses state of the art computer vision in mobile applications for faster information capture and retrieval. On June 23, 2010, Occipital sold its RedLaser product line to eBay. Occipital remains an independent company.

In December 2008, the situation for Occipital was dire. We had a $10,000 deferred legal bill, dried up personal bank accounts, and no revenue. Seven months earlier we had flown out to Boulder to join TechStars with little more than a prototype piece of software that could recognize the logos on paper receipts. In the first week, we realized that everybody thought the technology was cool, but otherwise hated the idea.

Then we found a sexier idea that everyone loved. We were going to build a huge, multiplatform consumer application that used artificial intelligence to solve the world's photo organization problems. There was a lot of buzz in our favor after we demonstrated an early prototype in September, but we failed to close funding for a number of reasons.

This failure gave us one major asset: a big chip on our shoulder. We didn't need anyone else's money. We already had what we needed, which was a core competency in computer vision, a technology area that we believed had incredible intrinsic value. In fact, we were borderline arrogant about it—we hypothesized that we could just hack off a tiny chunk of this technology and turn it into revenue. We tested this, stayed small, and launched ClearCam on February 3, 2009. ClearCam is a $10 iPhone application that captures high-resolution photos with the aid of computer vision. ClearCam was popular and we immediately were cash-flow positive. Near-death averted and hypothesis reinforced.

We got excited about going big again. But this time we wanted to become even bigger, which translated into technology that was an order of magnitude harder. That led to a near-merger with a group of seasoned entrepreneurs and another failed attempt at getting investors excited. The chip on our shoulder got bigger and led us to hack off a slightly larger chunk of technology than ClearCam. This turned into RedLaser, the first iPhone barcode scanner that really worked because it used computer vision to compensate for blur.

The response to our new product blew us away and RedLaser claimed a position in the top five paid applications on the iPhone App Store for many months. Today, we're more confident than ever about the technology area we have focused on, we have a growing reputation with consumers, and we have the money to stop worrying about the premature death of the company.

By staying tiny and taking incrementally harder technology steps, we saw Occipital's value increase dramatically. Now that we've found a formula that works, we are finally about to start growing our team from a stronger position than at any point in our history.

Jeff and his Occipital co-founder, Vikas Reddy, are the epitome of bootstrap entrepreneurs. Every TechStars class seems to have one and Occipital wins the bootstrapper of TechStars Boulder 2008 award. As you just read, they hunkered down and with no financing reinvented themselves several times until they launched RedLaser, which became a runaway hit. As Red-Laser took off, they had a set of interesting investment offers but no longer needed outside capital and chose not to take any of the offers.

While Jeff and Vikas were on their way to creating an interesting mobile e-commerce company, they wanted to work on a much bigger set of technical challenges than RedLaser in computer vision and augmented reality, their areas of passion and technical expertise. In their travels, they had a few inquiries for an acquisition of the company, but really only wanted to sell the RedLaser product, not the entire company. Fortunately, they found a buyer in eBay, which was very interested in the RedLaser product without requiring Jeff and Vikas to stay involved long term. Financial terms were quickly reached and eBay acquired RedLaser.

Given this sale, Occipital is now a long way from ever raising outside capital. Jeff and Vikas are now extremely well funded, are scaling up a very interesting team, and going after a huge vision. They stayed tiny and made sure they were "too small to fail" until they shouldn't be and it's paying off big for them.

Jeff Powers of Occipital and his co-founder Vikas Reddy take questions in 2008 at a Boulder New Tech Meetup.

Don't Celebrate the Wrong Things

Rob Johnson

Rob is a co-founder of EventVue, a company that helps conference organizers by providing an online community for the event and driving new conference registrations. EventVue raised $500,000 from angel investors after completing TechStars in 2007 but ultimately shut down.

All startups have too many available choices. It's the fundamental challenge of a startup—what customers to choose, what problem to solve, what flow to present to the user. Several methodologies have recently emerged, such as Eric Ries's lean startups to help guide you through the critical market and product decisions that drive you toward the promised land of hockey stick growth. But these methodologies fail to directly address an absolutely crucial component of doing a startup: how to keep everyone excited about your company.

In my firsthand experience with EventVue and my experience watching other TechStars companies, I've come to understand that the magic to keeping and growing momentum in your startup is knowing what to celebrate. If you celebrate what matters when it matters, your team, fans, and investors will push you forward. If you celebrate the wrong things, you'll wake up from the celebration no closer to success.

If acknowledging and marking the accomplishment of the right things is so important, how do you know what to celebrate? It's always tempting to celebrate the one-time events, and early in EventVue's life we did exactly that. We celebrated our first round of angel funding by hosting a funding party for all our investors, our team, and our friends. While it was an important milestone in our company's life, we weren't actually closer to being a significant company; we simply had more time to keep working. When we came back to work the day after our party we didn't have any more customers, users, or revenue than the previous day. While we had rallied enthusiasm and attention in a public way, we didn't have any actual progress to sustain it.

So if a first funding isn't always the moment of actual great celebration, surely customer growth is, right? Here again you must be careful. At EventVue, there had always been several tech conferences that we would drool over one day signing as customers. When the day finally came when we successfully closed one of these conferences, I went on a stage and announced it to an audience of current and future investors, took the team to dinner, and generally declared that we were now the market leader. We were proud of landing this prestigious customer and we were going to show it. What we failed to realize at the time was that we hadn't actually learned to grow the business. We were celebrating getting one customer but didn't know how to get the hundreds that we needed.

In each case, our celebrations were us saying to our team, investors, and market, "Here's what matters, and we've accomplished it!" This is implicit in any celebration and can pay huge dividends for you in energy, awareness, and momentum, if and only if you can actually continue to have progress. Without continued meaningful progress after celebrating, you've created a debt of energy, momentum, and credibility. Therefore, you must ensure that what you celebrate is actual progress toward a repeatable business.

Of course, everyone loves (and needs) positive feedback. You should definitely congratulate your team for a major code release, but save the champagne for the first month you meet your weekly ship date each week. Ring the sales bell for the big close, but save the party for the first consecutive quarters of making your targets.

How you celebrate will largely determine your company's culture. Make sure you celebrate the things that matter for the long haul.

Startups are hard and many fail. Rob and his co-founder Josh Fraser gave EventVue a good shot, but ultimately decided to shut it down. They wrote a very public and thoughtful post-mortem on their company blog announcing and explaining the decision and demonstrating that there is as much—and often more—to learn from failure than from success. The post-mortem follows:

Unfortunately, we have decided to shut down EventVue. We're very thankful for all the support that EventVue has received. Many people have helped us, cheered for us, and challenged us.

We also deeply believe in the power of failure to teach and help us learn. In fact, we understand with even more clarity now why there is so much advice for entrepreneurs—no one who has failed wants their mistakes repeated. In that spirit, we're sharing publicly our EventVue postmortem.

Over the past three years, we have tried various products and markets in the event industry and have not made a business with growth. The product that we used to raise our first round of funding was private social networks for events. During TechStars, we had an early nonpaying customer who deployed an EventVue social network for his conference of early adopter tech guys. We saw strong usage at this event and used those numbers to tell an investor story that led to our first angel round. At the time, we did not think about or understand the challenges of getting a lot of conference organizers to use EventVue. Internally, we had begun to think that we needed a stronger value prop for our customers than "we help your attendees meet more people" and so we pitched EventVue as a way to drive more attendees to events.

After our funding, instead of investing in the product features to deliver on EventVue directly driving people to events (hindsight: mistake), we immediately went out and tried to sell the social network tool to conference organizers. We had one-off victories by landing a few customers this way over the next nine months that kept us going. We had to invest product resources in rebuilding the site to handle the load from one or two high attendee events. However, because we were basically calling on friends of friends who ran events to be our customers, we didn't learn what event organizers in general wanted or how to acquire them as customers in a scalable way with the "private social network product."

We then realized the combination of a small price point (side effect of a nice-to-have value prop) and a long sales cycle (event organizers start planning their events six months or more beforehand), which meant that if we were to continue to do a direct enterprise sales model, we'd need to go after the big boys in the event industry—major tech publishers with hundreds of events. We hoped that with one signature we could get dozens of events. We made progress here and while we signed on some large customers, we never got the "enterprise-wide deal" that we hoped for. However, our strategy of "get big accounts" and some last-minute tenacity somehow got us to close our double-down round last Christmas, in the midst of the "RIP Good Times" chaos.

As the deals for the enterprise accounts began to drag on and on, we finally decided to do what we should have done much earlier. We decided to make our first major product pivot. At the VCIR conference last winter, we laid out a plan to build a product that would hopefully help deliver more attendees to conferences. At the time, we summarized our goals as: prove conference organizers will pay an affiliate fee for new attendees, prove that our widget will drive new attendees, and prove that we can get 100 event organizers to install our widget. Through the early summer we accomplished the first, built the widget (EventVue Discover), hit a giant brick wall on the second (Discover actually ended up losing money for our alpha customers), and never got to the third.

We never fully committed to Discover or the product pivot (hindsight: another mistake) and continued to sell our EventVue Community product for revenue to buy us more time. We began to notice that users of the community product actually enjoyed using our "chatter" feature that had somewhat real-time tweets about the conference. Since Discover was not working, we decided to simplify and focus EventVue on realtime conversation for events. Since November, we have built a widget version of a real-time event stream along with our hosted version. This was major product pivot Number 3.

We relaunched EventVue to be "best way to discuss events in real time" last week, focusing only on the chatter functionality that was popular in our social network. This was really a Hail Mary pass because we were out of capital and doing consulting work to buy time to get the relaunch out the door. Unfortunately, we have not seen enough traction to make us want to keep working on this. It really is too little, too late.

Our Deadly Strategic Mistakes

- We tried to build a sales effort too early, with too weak of a product after initial financing.
- We waited too long to address the "nice to have" problem.
- We went after enterprise sales model with a nonrecurring, small price.
- We didn't make EventVue self-serve to let anyone come and get it.

Our Deadly Cultural Mistakes

- We didn't focus on learning and failing fast until it was too late.
- We didn't care about or focus enough about discovering how to market EventVue.
- We made compromises in early hiring decisions, choosing expediency over talent and competency.

There are many more, but those are the ones that are forefront on our minds. Many of you have told us that failure is the most effective instructor and we definitely think that that has been the case with EventVue.

EventVue has been a fun journey. Thanks again to everyone who has supported us over the last few years.

Rob Johnson and Josh Fraser of EventVue at Boulder's monthly New Tech Meetup.

Be Specific

Brad Feld

Brad is a managing director at Foundry Group and one of the co-founders of TechStars.

A company I have a small investment in has been struggling to get the most recent version of their software shipped. A few weeks ago, I ran into the CEO, who grabbed me and said, "We are almost ready to go live." I looked at him and said, "When is the release?" His answer was "Friday."

I gave him a Bronx cheer and said, "When on Friday?" He looked at me like I was an alien. I clarified—"Do you mean 12:01 A.M. on Friday, 4:59 P.M. on Friday, or 11:59 P.M. on Friday?" I then clarified some more: "And I mean in Mountain Time." We agreed that 11:59 P.M. on Friday was a good time (which they missed, but they got it out a few days later).

At my first company (Feld Technologies), our client base got to the point where we were often doing multiple releases of different software on a weekly basis. We were a custom software company but used a very traditional software engineering approach to our projects. For a long time, we used dates to mark releases (for example, "Friday"). After way too many 11:59 P.M. releases when our clients were definitely not sticking around the office to wait for us and missed FedEx deadlines (this was back when you had to FedEx the disks to the clients in another state because modems were too slow to transmit the files), we learned that a release has both a date and a time. We also learned that the external release is, at the minimum, the date plus one of the internal release, especially on systems with live data. We also learned that the only appropriate days of the week for a release are Tuesday, Wednesday, or Thursday. I'll let you guess as to why this is.

As I work with new startups and first-time entrepreneurs, I see people learning this lesson over and over again. I think it's just going to be part of the endless education of new software entrepreneurs that you never really learn until you are in the real world. It's important to be specific, not just concerning release dates, but also for everything that you commit to doing.

Learn from Your Failures

Fred Wilson

Fred is a managing partner at Union Square Ventures and is an investor in companies including Twitter, Zynga, and Foursquare. Fred has been a TechStars mentor since 2008.

Photo Courtesy of Union Square Ventures

> *You can't let your failures define you—you have to let them teach you.*
> *You have to let them show you what to do differently next time.*
> —Barack Obama in his "back to school speech."

That's so true. It took me a while to learn that lesson.

When I first started out in the venture capital business, I was afraid to make a mistake. Once I started investing and taking board seats myself, I worked super hard to avoid losing money. I went for almost a decade without making a losing investment.

Then, in the aftermath of the Internet bubble, the wheels came off the bus. We wrote off close to 20 investments in the span of two years from late 2000 to late 2002. It was devastating on many levels.

But when I look back on my career, it is not the successes that I think back on most. It is the failures, and particularly those two years when everything that could go wrong did go wrong.

When my partner Brad Burnham and I started Union Square Ventures in 2003, we laid out a roadmap for what kind of firm we wanted to create, what kind of investments we'd make, and how we thought the Internet was going to evolve. That work was largely a result of the lessons we both had learned in the aftermath of the bubble.

I think embracing failure is one of the things that makes this country such a great place to do business in. In many parts of the world, if you fail once, you are done. People won't touch you with a 10-foot pole. But here in the United States, it's almost a badge of honor. And our president explains why.

When we meet with entrepreneurs, I'm always interested in their failures. And most people have them; you just have to dig a bit to find them. If someone has failed and taken the time to learn from it, I think that's a big positive. It makes us even more excited to back them the next time.

So don't hide your failures. Wear them as a badge of honor. And most of all, learn from them.

Fred Wilson (left) at the 2008 TechStars Boulder Demo Day, catching up with Jason Mendelson of Foundry Group and Alex White of Next Big Sound.

Fred's essay originally appeared on his blog at avc.com.

Quality over Quantity

Andy Smith

Andy is the co-founder and CEO of DailyBurn, the premier fitness social network for detailed tracking, online accountability, and motivation. DailyBurn raised $500,000 from angel investors after completing TechStars in 2008. They were acquired by IAC in 2010.

Photo Courtesy of ThisWeekIn.com

Feature creep. The sound of those words should scare you to death.

If you are a technical founder, please listen carefully: You don't need to build a bunch of new features to make your startup successful. Trust me, I know.

Both of the founders of DailyBurn (we were called Gyminee while we were at TechStars) are technology geeks. Naturally, our instinct is to always look at our product, see what is missing, and then try to quickly build the next killer feature that will magically get all of our users to convert to paying users. It's a problem facing all startups, but especially startups that are filled with developers.

Most technical founders have the skills to quickly build a ton of features. It isn't hard for us to bang out some code and get the thing up and running on the web site within hours. But many of these features don't matter and often detract from the product.

So what is the secret behind building useful, meaningful features?

First, focus on ease of use. Your site and your new features have to be very easy to use and graphically appealing. If you try to rush out a ton of features, it will not look good and will result in an unpolished, and hard to use product. One of the things we are most proud of about DailyBurn is that we've made the product look good while being very easy to use. We realize that a site to track your workouts and food intake isn't an earth-shattering idea and that there are a lot of sites out there trying to do the same thing we do. The reason we have been able to grow is because we make it as easy as possible for users to track their fitness on our site.

Next, build one thing well. If you try to build every feature that comes to mind, the result will be an unfocused product with no chance of success. When we started DailyBurn we focused on one thing and one thing only—a social workout tracking tool that lets you track actual results. We did that one thing well, got an audience, and then listened to our users. User after user screamed for food and nutrition tracking, so we took our time and built high quality nutrition tracking. Now our food-tracking tool is even more popular than our workout tracking tools because we focused on quality.

Finally, listen to some, but not all, of your users. User feedback is good, but don't listen to all of it. We had so many early requests for features (and we still get hundreds a day) that we would have drowned if we tried to implement a fraction of them. You have to be willing to say no to your users.

Want to know a secret? The next new big feature you are working on will only convert a marginal number of new users to paying users and not be your big ticket to acquisition next week. In fact, that big feature you are working on right now might be a complete bust and you could lose users. Measure the impact of every new feature so you'll know for sure what kind of effect each of them has.

Focus on quality—not just quantity. And make something that makes you proud (not just your mom).

The quality over quantity approach has governed TechStars' expansion to other cities. When TechStars started in Boulder, we didn't know if it would work. After the first year, we had lots of inquiries from other entrepreneurs and angel investors about starting up a TechStars program in other cities in the United States. We considered this, decided we had a lot to get right about the program before we were ready to expand, and decided only to do a Boulder program in Year Two.

Source: Photo Courtesy of Wade Simmons.

Andy Smith presents Gyminee (now DailyBurn) at TechStars Boulder 2008 Demo Day.

While the first year of TechStars was great, the second year was phenomenal. Once again, we received many inbound inquiries about starting TechStars in other cities. We encouraged other folks to do this themselves, open sourced the TechStars program by sharing our ideas, documents, and approach, but decided to stay focused on Boulder.

Along the way, we were approached by Bill Warner about doing a TechStars program in Boston. Given Brad's long history in Boston, this was a lot more comfortable than trying to start up a program in a city we didn't know. And Bill was the definition of quality—we knew that if he were involved, our effort would be serious and well executed. So we decided to branch out and opened the second TechStars program in Boston in our third year.

After the third Boulder program and the first Boston program, we were inundated with requests for programs in additional cities. We thought hard about this, realizing that if we wanted to expand faster, it was conceivable that there was the demand for at least 50 Tech-Stars programs in just the United States. While we saw many other programs getting started, we were really concerned about quality. As a result, we decided that it was always going to be more important to us to do a high quality job and help create a high percentage of great startups than it would be to go after quantity. At that point we made a decision that the core TechStars program could be at most four cities.

This focus on quality has generated other interesting opportunities for TechStars, some of which—such as the TechStars Global Affiliate program—are starting to roll out. By continuing to focus on quality, we say no to a lot of opportunities but when we decide to go after something, we are confident we can do it well. We think all startups should think this way.

Have a Bias Toward Action

Ben Casnocha

Ben is an entrepreneur and author of the book My Startup Life: What a (Very) Young CEO Learned on His Journey Through Silicon Valley. *He has been a TechStars mentor since 2007.*

Learning experts agree that learning by doing is the best way to learn something. When you do something—when you pick up the phone and talk to a potential customer, launch a prototype, send out the first brochure—you learn infinitely more than if you think about doing it in the abstract. The best way to test the validity of a business idea, for example, is to start the business and quickly gauge market feedback.

The best entrepreneurs have internalized learn-by-doing to the bone. As my friend Josh Newman says, there are only two steps to entrepreneurship: start, and keep going—and you lose most people at the first step. That's because talk is easy. Writing business plans is easy. Chatting about your business idea with friends at a party is easy. Taking an action—starting, doing—is hard.

It's hard because when you take an action, it may turn out to have been the wrong action. Fine. When you have a bias toward action, it means you are constantly making decisions, and some of those decisions will surely have bad outcomes. But good decisions can have bad outcomes. Intel founder Andy Grove says the key to business success is to make lots of decisions and correct course very quickly when you realize you're wrong. Always be acting, and with confidence, but always be ready to iterate and evolve your thinking if you discover you made the wrong move.

It's hard because you'll play games with yourself. Sometimes you might think, "If I wait just a little bit longer, I'll get more information that will allow me to make a better decision." No! General Colin Powell told his commanders in the Army that he expected them to make decisions on 40 percent of available information. Consider this when you next think you need more time to figure out whether you should start your business, launch the new product, or pick up the phone and call that CEO you respect.

It's hard because self-discipline is hard. To take an action requires the self-discipline to actually sit down and do a thing. So let others discipline you. Tell friends and family what you plan to do, and ask them to hold your feet to the fire. External accountability works wonders.

Ben Casnocha talks to the 2008 TechStars companies about thinking differently.

But don't take it from me.

Herb Kelleher, the founder of Southwest Airlines, says, "We have a strategic plan. It's called doing things." As an entrepreneur, you should substitute "business plan" in place of "strategic plan" and then sit and deeply ponder.

Bill Parcells, the NFL football coach, posts a sign in the locker room before every game: "Blame Nobody. Expect Nothing. Do Something." Even the most elite athletes in the world need to be reminded to do stuff!

Mark Twain said, "We regret the things we don't do more than the things we do." The question "I wonder what would have happened if . . ." hurts more than a bad outcome.

So what are you waiting for?

Do or Do Not, There Is No Try

Brad Feld

Brad is a managing director at Foundry Group and one of the co-founders of TechStars.

When I grow up I want to be like Yoda (except for the short green part). Until then, I'll just do my best to incorporate his philosophy into my life.

```
$DO || ! $DO; try
Try: command not found
```

I've always found this Yoda quote to epitomize how I try to live my life. Ever since I was a little kid, I never really understood what *try* meant. There were lots of things I did and lots of things I failed at. However, even when I failed, I viewed myself as having "done it" even if I wasn't successful. When I wanted to master something, I did it a lot. I didn't try to do it—I did it, and accepted the failure along with the success.

Throughout the years I heard many people say, "You should try this" or "You should try that." Sometimes it was trivial (for example, you should try foie gras); other times, it was complex (you should try to learn how to play the piano.) My parents taught me early on that "No" or "I'm not interested" was an acceptable answer, so I was rarely intimidated when faced with something new. I also started to understand the difference between *preference* (for example, try foie gras and see if you like it) and *accomplishment* (try to learn how to play the piano). I realized preference was unimportant in the context of accomplishment but the inverse mattered—namely that accomplishment was important in the context of preference. Specifically, you could accomplish a wide range of things whether you had a preference for them, but that when you tried to accomplish that thing, it mattered a lot whether you had a preference for it.

Now, ponder the phrase "You should try entrepreneurship." What exactly does that really mean? How about "You should try to start a company." Or "You should try to build a product." Or even "You should try to sell something to someone." Try? Really? If you have a preference for entrepreneurship, or think you have a preference for entrepreneurship, just go for it. You might fail—but that's okay and is part of the process. If you start a company that ultimately fails, you are still an entrepreneur. And your next step should be to go start another company.

If you don't have a preference for entrepreneurship (or—more specifically—entrepreneurship doesn't interest you), you have no business creating a company in the first place. Starting a company is extremely hard and requires commitment on many levels. Ultimately, you don't really "try to start a company"—you either do it or you don't.

Do or do not—there is no try.

THEME 4: PRODUCT

From an outsider's perspective, startups are often synonymous with their products. After all, that's the only connection most people will ever have to your company. It therefore follows that if your product sucks, your company sucks. And I'm sure you'll agree that the majority of products, at least on the Internet, suck. You do the math.

We often talk about the Number One startup killer at TechStars—making a product for which there is no interesting market. TechStars accepts just 10 of more than 600 startups that apply and presumably they are among the best. But still, we find that at least one-third of those startups are attempting to build a product that they want, or that no one wants, instead of what the market wants. Every year, this is one of the key things that happens at TechStars—products get dropped, and new ones are born. You can't hide from a lack of market at TechStars. It stalks you and threatens to kill you.

The best entrepreneurs we know are obsessed with their products. Dick Costolo, currently the COO of Twitter and previously the CEO of FeedBurner, wakes up each morning with his product on his mind. Rob Hayes of First Round Capital talks about how to pivot when your product isn't working. And Eric Marcoullier, the founder of MyBlogLog, Gnip, and OneTrueFan reminds us to regularly throw things away.

You'll find that much of this section is about how to get to the right product, not about the tactics of building what you imagine the right product to be. That, as they say, is a feature and not a bug.

Don't Wait Until You Are Proud of Your Product

Ajay Kulkarni and Andy Cheung

Ajay and Andy are co-founders of Sensobi, a company that makes better mobile address books, and completed TechStars in 2009.

Startups are like music bands—without fans (or users or customers), you don't have much. At first, we thought building a business was a linear process: build the product, charge for it, and people will pay you. If you're launching a business in a known industry with a known product, like a coffee shop, you can follow that model. But tech entrepreneurs don't live in that world: we live to innovate and to build a new product that transforms an existing industry or creates a whole new industry.

If you are innovating, you actually don't know what your product needs to be. Furthermore, your customers don't either. No one does. But what you do know is that there is a problem that the right product will solve. It's through rapid iteration—trial and error—that you can figure this out. You're basically running experiments, and for these particular experiments you need test subjects. You need users, especially the kind who want to experiment alongside you because they believe in your vision.

When we started at TechStars, we had a working demo but no users. We thought we had a good idea of who our target user was. Our goal with our product was to help professionals stay on top of their important relationships. We initially thought salespeople would need our application the most; this had a big influence on our product roadmap and our positioning. We even designed a persona around the sales professional.

Then with Shawn Broderick, the managing director of TechStars Boston, cracking his whip at our backs, we launched our beta. A lot of different types of people downloaded the app. We tracked usage, ran surveys, interviewed our power users, and iterated with new releases every two weeks. To our surprise, only a few of the core group of early users who loved our app and used it every day were salespeople. Yet everyone who used it saw the value in having stronger personal relationships.

Our early beta users helped us realize that there were a variety of professionals out there who relied on personal relationships for their business, and very few of them were actually in sales. This caused us to reconsider our product and marketing plans with this broader base in mind.

We're still an early pre-revenue startup and haven't entirely figured this out yet, but we have realized that we don't know what we don't know. And it's only through conversations with our users that we are going to figure it out.

You need to have the discipline to let your product go, warts and all, into the world. For the perfectionists in the room, you have to cut yourself off from the temptation of adding just one more thing. When you are your own boss, it's so easy to push off the release date. Don't do it. As our mentor Dharmesh Shah told us, "If you aren't releasing your crappy bug-laden product, you're too late."

Having a great product doesn't mean that you hold on to it for years and years and polish it endlessly. As Ajay and Andy point out, releasing early and often is the key to figuring out how to make your product great. They weren't afraid to get their early version out there, and when they did, they learned more from the experiences their users had than they would from months of internal discussions about what their users might want.

At TechStars, we encourage everyone to use an agile software development methodology, using a real agile project management tool from a company such as Rally Software, with product releases at least every two weeks. A few companies manage to get to the nirvana of continuous development, where they deploy changes to their application many times a day. Regardless of the approach, getting your product into the hands of your users quickly, with regular updates, is a key to getting to a great product.

Find Your Whitespace

Raj Aggarwal

Raj is a co-founder and CEO of Localytics, a provider of mobile application analytics. Localytics raised $700,000 from angel investors after completing TechStars in 2009.

While companies with monopolies don't worry much about differentiation, startups are not afforded that luxury. Nearly every startup must find ways to differentiate itself from competitors, whether it's through location, service, price, product features, or something else. As your competition increases, so does your need to differentiate. This becomes even more critical in a crowded market, as your product's differentiation needs to clear enough to help you rise above the noise.

In the midst of the financial crisis in the fall of 2008 and spring of 2009, very few people were thinking about hot new market segments. There were a few notable ones, however, including the fulfillment of the longtime promise of the smart phone. Kickstarted by the Apple iPhone and the App Store in early 2008, developers were busily creating apps for this new platform. We created Localytics to provide analytics to these mobile app developers. We initially set out to address a need we saw in this market, which was that the analytical data about usage of mobile apps was lousy. We worked closely with several mobile app makers from Day One, understanding what they wanted and what they were willing to pay for, and created a service to address their needs.

Over the next several months, new competitors entered the market. Each new company caused us some anguish and sparked questions about the viability of our business. On inspection of the competitive solutions, it was clear competitors were going after the middle and long tail of the market and we could differentiate ourselves at the top end of the market. The needs of large brands and enterprises creating apps are unique and we refocused our efforts to address their needs. While it is still early and the mobile analytics market is still emerging, our differentiation is strong enough that many of the top app publishers have chosen to work with us.

When we look back on what we did to find our whitespace, it came down to a few things. First, we identified a target market and researched it by speaking to as many people in it as we could. Through this we found some early enthusiastic customers and developed a product to meet their specific needs. We iterated with them frequently and weren't afraid of redefining our product or segment focus based on their feedback. This process made it clear that our competitors were not addressing the needs of top app publishers and we focused all of our product, marketing, and sales efforts on them. After getting over our initial concern about competitors, we didn't worry about them. Instead, we learned as much as we could about them to make sure that we were articulating our differences—specifically why we were better for certain customers.

Creating a startup in a crowded market can be intimidating and the typical ups and downs any startup experiences will be amplified. Realize that the reason your market is crowded is that there is big growth opportunity. If you understand your customers and your competitors well enough, it usually becomes obvious what your whitespace is and what you'll need to do to exploit it.

As part of finding their whitespace, Raj and his team did something we encourage every TechStars teams to do—they obsessed about their competitors, but weren't afraid of them. From the beginning, Raj studied the products of each of his competitors. He built relationships with them, talked to them, and explored ways to collaborate with them. While he didn't know what would come of this, at the minimum he got to understand them better, which helped him more clearly define his whitespace.

We often encounter entrepreneurs who mythologize their competitors. Rather than try to understand them and relate to them, they make up stories in their minds about them. They believe everything they read on blogs, allow rumor and innuendo to define them, and attribute behavior, aspirations, and goals to them as a result.

In many cases, your competitors don't even know you exist. This gives you a huge advantage as an early stage startup because you can learn from what they are doing and how they are talking about the market and their customers, while approaching things from a different perspective. At the same time, don't be afraid to reach out to them and get to know them. Where it leads might surprise you.

Raj Aggarwal and the Localytics team in Boston, 2009.

Focus on What Matters

Dick Costolo

Dick is the COO of Twitter and was previously the co-founder and CEO of Feed-Burner, which was acquired by Google in 2007. Dick has been a TechStars mentor since 2007.

Photo by Kenneth Yeung, thelettertwo.com

I t is very easy to lose your focus at a company of any size; to go chase some shiny object instead of making sure you have nailed down the single most important thing. This is most dangerous when you are a small company starting to gain traction. People are calling you! Other companies know who you are! Journalists know who you are! At this point in your company's life, there are numerous opportunities to lose focus coming at you every day. Large financial opportunities appear that are off strategy but have big revenue attached to them. Strategic opportunities that are not central to what you are doing, but possibly could provide real lift and momentum to your business, show up at your doorstep. Each day you think about all the progress you could make if you just changed some of your priorities for next week, next month, and next quarter.

When FeedBurner was starting to become popular in 2005, and we'd hired our first director of business development, Rick Klau (now running Blogger at Google), he would occasionally come to my desk and say, "Company X will pay us an extraordinary amount of money to do this thing with their feeds. We've never really talked about that before but it could be a good opportunity and it's really a ton of money." My reaction, which eventually became Rick's reaction, was "Do we have all the feeds yet? No? Okay, then let's just focus on getting all the feeds. Step One is to get all the feeds. Don't bring me a rabbit; bring me more feeds. Throw away the rabbits."

What I meant here was that our first job as a company was to gain market share. We had a few competitors and we knew that a media opportunity around advertising would demand significant market share. At our young stage as a company, market share and market penetration mattered a lot. It's easy to say you are going to focus on what you set out to do, but you have to have the courage to stay focused when you are spending money and there are exciting revenue opportunities that pop up in front of you. If you have a plan and you haven't yet seen that the plan doesn't work, then stay on plan and execute as quickly as possible so you can test the hypothesis of the plan.

Focusing on what matters doesn't mean that you should be obstinate about your strategy and never change it. The key is to test the hypotheses of your plan as quickly as possible so that you can understand if and when you need to change course. When I would tell Rick "First, get all the feeds," what I really meant was "First, get enough of a critical mass of feeds to test the advertising hypothesis." Once we'd tested that, we redoubled our focus on "getting all the feeds" and began to have a second team work on iterating the advertising model.

It is too easy to think there are nine things you should be doing as a company when you should really probably be doing only two or three. Always trim away what you don't need to be doing and ask yourself, "What is the thing that matters most to making progress right now?" Focus on these and let the other bright ideas sit on the sidelines until the company has proven that it's ready to tackle another opportunity.

Obsess over Metrics

Dave McClure

Dave is an angel investor and has been geeking out in Silicon Valley for almost 20 years as a software developer, entrepreneur, startup advisor, blogger, and Internet marketing nerd. He's been a TechStars mentor since 2007.

The ability to get real-time data and feedback is unique to the Internet. If you're smart, you can take advantage of that and build better products by collecting real-time usage metrics and by making decisions based on measured user data.

Today, you are probably building too much stuff and you are also probably measuring too much stuff. Contrary to popular belief, engineering is generally not the most important thing in an Internet business. You've probably engineered too much already and there are probably features that you should remove from your product. What's really hard is simplifying your product and building a great user experience.

It's important to start by building a culture of feedback and measured analytics into your process and your organization. The reason for this is that startup success often boils down to your ability to do two things: make money and make users happy. If you can figure out how to do both of those things at scale, then you probably have an interesting business on your hands. Luckily, you can tell if users are happy or not by measuring their behavior.

There are five key metrics to measuring user behavior and happiness:

1. Acquisition—How are users coming to your site through various channels?
2. Activation—Are users happy with their first experience?
3. Retention—Are users coming back?
4. Referral—Are users telling others?
5. Revenue—Are users spending money or allowing you to monetize in some way?

In case you need any help remembering these metrics, the first letters spell AARRR! and are at the core of my presentation (which you can find on the Web) about Startup Metrics for Pirates.

Every year Dave makes a trip out to Boulder and spends a day with each of the TechStars teams. In addition to encouraging them to think like pirates, he gives them all a rapidfire dose of product feedback from someone who has probably looked at as many products on the Web as anyone on the planet.

Dave's insights are powerful while always trending back to a core set of questions—is this going to delight your users and will they tell everyone they know? If they will, you'll win. If they won't, you won't.

Avoid Distractions

Andy Sack

Andy is the managing director of Tech-Stars in Seattle, the co-founder of Founders Co-op, and the co-founder of Revenue Loan.

Photo by Randy Stewart

I became the lead investor in Tom Staple's company, Cooler Planet, in July 2007. The company was originally conceived to do lead generation in the energy efficiency market. Neither Tom, Chris DeVore (my partner at Founders Co-Op), nor I had experience in anything remotely related to the energy efficiency market. We didn't let that ignorance stop us; we were knowledgeable about online marketing and we thought the trend toward green energy was going to grow a bunch over the next five years.

Tom decided to focus on and win the solar market first. His theory was that energy efficiency was too broad a market to cover; solar was narrower and it'd be easier for us to matter to both consumers and merchants if we narrowed our focus. At first, Tom thought that winning the solar market would take about six months. We were right about narrowing our focus but totally underestimated the time that it would take to win the solar market.

Tom spent the first two years building a series of web sites that provided the backbone of becoming the Number One consumer resource for solar information online. The business model is simple: The company attracts user traffic interested in solar (both paid and organic) and then monetizes the traffic by selling leads to solar installers.

Over the last two years, we've had regular conversations about expanding into other submarkets in the energy efficient market such as energy audits, HVAC, wind, and geothermal. Every time we've had the conversation about expanding to a different or broader market, one way or another we've decided to stay focused on winning solar. The consideration of diverting our scarce resources, namely time, money, and focus, to other markets forced us to determine what winning in the solar market meant. Ultimately, we came up with a concrete metric for what winning the market meant—we needed to rank in the top five organic search results for the top five keyword terms such as *solar power.*

We've been forced to work hard to achieve that metric. We've occasionally wondered if it was the right goal or if we should have expanded our business sooner. We've also wondered if we were in the wrong business altogether or if we even had a business.

We usually entertained conversations of switching goals and markets most when we lacked confidence in our vision because current results were not as big or coming as fast as we wanted. But every time we wondered, we came back to focusing on the goal and winning the traffic and search engine game for solar. We knew that if we achieved that position online, then a lot of companies would be interested in paying us money. We also believed we would be able to command a large premium in the market for being Number One online in the solar business.

At the beginning of 2010 while we were making the annual operating plan for the company, we once again had the conversation about expanding the business by going into a new market. We figured we had some final housekeeping to do on one of our solar web sites and we would then start our expansion. We conducted simple multivariate testing on this web site and within a few days increased conversion by 40 percent. This blew our minds—we knew that if these simple tweaks could improve performance this much, we had a lot more work to do before we expanded into a new market.

I've found that to make the decision to focus on one area instead of expanding into several is a tough one. Like many decisions in early stage companies, it comes down to part instinct and part assessment. Building an early stage business requires many moments of scratching one's head and then putting one's head down again and executing only to lift it up again to see what has been accomplished. Defining an achievable and worthwhile goal (for example, being among the top five in keywords on Google) was helpful. Staying with that goal has enabled us to persevere through the ups and downs and the inevitable wonderings of "Wouldn't life be easier if we did something else?"

Cooler Planet is two years old, and when we look back at how dumb we were at the beginning in the way we did things it's amazing we're still in business. We've been rewarded every time we've decided not to switch markets and to stay focused on bootstrapping our business. We remain singularly focused on being Number One online in the solar market and we continue to think that that will take us about six months to achieve that goal!

Andy and his partners at Cooler Planet threw away the same rabbits that Dick Costolo did when he was focusing on what matters. It's so easy to be distracted by a new market, a new potential customer, or a new competitor. Instead, by having a clear goal ("have all the feeds," "be among the top five in all keywords for solar") you can regularly determine if you've achieved a definitive leadership position. As an early stage company, you should make sure you own your hill before you go try to conquer another one.

Know Your Customer

Bill Flagg

Bill is the former co-owner and president of RegOnline, a company that provides online registration software, and is currently an investor through his fund, The Felix Fund. He has been a TechStars mentor since 2007.

A real business boils down to one thing—serving peoples' needs and getting paid for it in a way that you can operate profitably. The best way to do that is to know your customers.

At RegOnline we constantly listened to what our customers needed and wanted. This process started with my business partner Attila who built the first version of our software on the basis of what one of our early customers requested. Attila then turned to the next customer, and the next customer, and the next customer until we had 5,000 happy ones.

Over time we began to expand our sales and marketing activities to be self-serve, through which our customer didn't have to talk to a salesperson to sign up for our service. We constantly looked for how we could make it easier for prospects to find what they wanted in our product by listening to what they asked the salespeople on the phones and then repeating that information in a simple way online.

Getting inside my prospects' and customers' minds was one of the most valuable activities I did at RegOnline. Getting face to face at trade shows helped me learn and play back what customers wanted. Sitting in on our public online demos to hear the questions prospects asked helped me get in their heads and understand what they were thinking. We did usability testing to see where our prospects and customers would trip up and fall when trying to do business with us. We'd take all of this information and iterate like crazy on the stuff that confused people or simply didn't work the way they expected. Our ultimate goal was to create a completely frictionless experience for our customers, resulting in a situation in which it was easy for them to fall in love with our service and with us.

We wanted our customers to know that we respected the idea that we were in business to serve them and that we didn't expect to get paid if we didn't do it correctly. We decided to put a message on our invoice that said "If you are not completely satisfied with your service, mark down this bill as you feel it is appropriate and tell us where we can improve."

Bill Flagg (seated, right) helping out Ignighter during the Summer of 2008.

There are so many distractions that we face as entrepreneurs—building cool technology, getting funding, hiring the right people, renting office space, creating partnerships, dealing with acquirers—that it's easy to lose sight of the reason we are in business. Make sure you stay focused and listen to what people need and help them get it. Then do that again, and again, and again.

Beware the Big Companies

Michael Zeisser

Michael is senior vice president of Liberty Media Corporation and has been a Tech-Stars mentor since 2008.

Entrepreneurs at TechStars often ask how big companies can help startups. An endorsement from a big company in the form of a distribution agreement or a partnership can be hugely valuable. Big companies can bring money, access to customers, and reputational benefits to your company as long as the big company doesn't accidentally kill you in the process.

I have witnessed startups overinvesting in developing a relationship with a big company. They poured too much time and attention into developing a deal, and although the deal ultimately materialized, its benefit fell far short of expectations. In discussions with big companies, it is very easy for entrepreneurs to develop "happy ears," the tendency to hear what one wants to hear, while overlooking the signals that suggest otherwise. My advice for startups is to be merciless in dealing with big companies. Yes, they can be your friends, but they can also destroy you.

The problem is that the risk is completely imbalanced. Whether something happens will typically not make a huge difference for the big company, whereas it could be a matter of life and death for the startup. While there is no fail-safe way to protect yourself, there are a few key pitfalls to avoid.

First, find the real decision maker. Most people in big companies have very little authority to make decisions although they don't like to admit it. For someone to succeed in a big company, conforming is usually more important than achieving results, so big company people will rarely tell you an inconvenient truth and almost never say no. If you are not getting straight answers, you are not talking to a decision maker and the big company is likely telling you "no" in its own language.

Next, realize that you cannot create the need. Entrepreneurs are by nature evangelists—they think they can change the world. Believing that you only need one more meeting or one more phone call to convince the big company that it needs to do business with you is understandable, but it is a huge mistake. You will end up spending much too much time trying to build a relationship that will be futile 99.9 percent of the time. Don't fool yourself.

Finally, fail fast. The biggest mistake startups make when dealing with a big company is to be blinded by whatever shiny brass ring they are pursuing and to fail to consider the opportunity cost associated with not pursuing alternatives. Opportunity cost can kill a startup. When dealing with a big company, you should have a vigilant discipline to align invested efforts and expected outcomes. When these two factors get out of alignment, the startup is taking on too great of a risk. Yes, occasionally there are Hail Mary passes, but relying on them is no way to build a company.

Many startups have benefited from using the shoulders of giants as a springboard for growth. But risks and incentives are usually not aligned between startups and big companies. The startup should approach opportunities in a spirit of partnership but never let happy ears get in the way of facing the music.

Virtually all large companies have people with titles like "Vice President of Corporate Development" or "Senior Vice President of Business Development." In many cases, the actual role is "Vice President of Not Corporate Development" or "Senior Vice President of Keeping Entrepreneurs Away From the People in BigCo that Actually Get Things Done." These people are often fun to hang out with, charming, and will fill you full of hope and excitement. But they rarely can get something done with a startup unless someone on the product and sales side of BigCo demands it. As Michael says, Beware.

Throw Things Away

Eric Marcoullier

Eric is the co-founder and CEO of OneTrue-Fan. He previously co-founded Gnip and was the co-founder and CEO of My-BlogLog, which was acquired by Yahoo! in 2007. He has been a TechStars mentor since 2007.

Photo Courtesy of WonderMill.com

In late September of 2009, I met with Gnip board member and lead investor Brad Feld. It had been a few weeks since we'd spoken face to face and the meeting quickly turned into a litany of reasons why I was stressed about the company. I felt like we were headed for insolvency in 12 months and I was powerless to fix it. When Brad mentioned that I sounded pretty unhappy, I threw caution to the wind and told him just how miserable I was. And suddenly, I found myself resigning as CEO.

I had not begun the meeting with that intention, but as I spelled out the sense of inertia that had taken over Gnip, it seemed like the logical decision. We had tried multiple times to expand on the core tech platform, and every time, it appeared that we weren't making progress. I felt like we had more drama than companies many times our size. And I was bored out of my mind with what I was doing on a daily basis. During the meeting with Brad, I spontaneously decided it was time for me to go.

Brad and I discussed the repercussions of leaving and they all sounded better to me than crash landing a company for the next 12 months. We parted that day with the understanding that I would take 36 hours and reconsider my decision. Afterward, we would get back together and sort out next steps for Gnip.

That night I went home and told my wife I was leaving the company. I started reaching out to friends who might help me find some consulting work to ease the sudden loss of income. I reached out to several other friends to inquire about startup ideas that had been rolling around in their heads. I was leaving Gnip.

But an interesting thing happened the next day. When compared to that most drastic step a founder can take, Gnip's problems suddenly seemed very small. An inflexible technology stack hamstrung us? Burn it to the ground and start over. The handpicked team that kept building variations of the tech stack? They could be let go. Our existing customer base? The recurring monthly revenue, while not inconsequential, didn't come close to achieving break even. We could nuke that, too. The product vice president that I hired was awesome but he was essentially filling a role that I desperately wanted and needed to fill. He could be let go, too.

I called Brad and hashed it out with him. Then I called Gnip's other investors and talked them through what I was thinking. An exchange with First Round Capital's Rob Hayes summed up the go forward plan:

Rob: So do you know whether there's a business here?

Me: We still don't have a clue, but I know that we can find out a hell of a lot faster if we make these changes.

Four days later I met with the team and laid off seven of Gnip's twelve employees. I sat down with the remaining team members and we started from scratch. We were going after solving the same problem, but with a completely new approach. Within six weeks, we built more new features than in the previous six months. At the three-month mark we were signing new customers and hiring additional team members. Things were back on track.

Each decision made in a startup creates indelible history that colors all future actions. In the best of times, it creates a corporate culture that enables flexibility. In the worst of times, it creates handcuffs that keep a company from responding to the daily lessons that a startup learns. It's easy to feel trapped by these handcuffs but if you change your perspective just a little, you might find that your hands are bound by nothing more than air, and the future is yours to create.

About six months later, Brad and Eric had another meeting. This time Gnip was in a much better place, but Eric was once again unhappy. Unlike the last time, it had nothing to do with where Gnip was at. Rather, it had to do with the type of business Gnip was.

Gnip provides web infrastructure to help aggregate social media. This is a highly technical problem, and as a result Gnip is akin to a plumbing business because they provide software wiring and data communication between other web services. Gnip's customers were web services—both consumer and business oriented—that needed to deal with social data.

Eric Marcoullier working with DailyBurn during the summer of 2008.

On the other hand, Eric had realized he was most happy in a consumer-facing Internet business. He was bored interacting with Gnip's customers and wanted instead to be interacting with the end users that Gnip's customers were working with. But, in the context of the business that was Gnip, this wasn't possible.

Fortunately, Eric had a strong technical co-founder who also had solid management experience. While Eric's partner, Jud Valeski, hadn't been a CEO before, most of the Gnip team was engineering focused and already reporting to Jud. After several days of thoughtful discussion, Eric decided to leave Gnip, and handed the reins to Jud.

Under Jud's leadership, Gnip is continuing to grow nicely. While it's still a young company, their product relevance and market timing is excellent. They solve a complex problem for their customers and, as a highly technical team, do it extremely well.

Eric is also in a much happier place. He's started a new company called OneTrueFan which is off to a fast start serving exactly the end users he wanted to serve. He's still a shareholder in Gnip and good friends with Brad, Jud, and his other investors. And he keeps showing up at TechStars and encouraging people to not be afraid to throw things away.

Pivot

Rob Hayes

Rob is a partner at First Round Capital and has been a TechStars mentor since 2008.

There is one thing that the hundred of founders I meet each year have in common, and that is that their plan is wrong. Sometimes it's the big things, sometimes it's the little things, but the plan is always wrong. Founders who can pivot to a new idea given what they learn will survive their plan being wrong while those who believe that all signs pointing to trouble are wrong are not going to survive.

My favorite example of a great pivot is from a company originally called Riya. This company had developed leading edge facial recognition technology at the same time that tagged photo sites like Flickr were becoming dominant. With Riya, you could point to someone's face in several pictures and tell the service who that person was. Riya would then find all instances of that person in all your photos and tag them with the appropriate person's name.

It turns out that the service worked fine but there was not as much user uptake as the company wanted. It became less clear pretty soon that there was a large, thriving business that could be built around this technology.

That did not deter the founder, Munjal Shah. He pivoted quickly and repurposed the technology toward a concept called "visual shopping" and rebranded the company as Like.com. It turns out that while hard goods like consumer electronics generally have enough meta-data around them to easily index for search (model numbers, brand names) most soft goods are much tougher to index ("a rug with blue flowers on it"). Riya (now Like.com's) technology could be used to solve this problem. Like.com allowed users to search for things that look like other things; users could even upload pictures of things they want to search for and Like.com would find similar items.

Munjal pivoted perfectly and since this pivot, the company has been doing very well.* His lessons are those that every founder should follow—start with a solid plan, but always listen to your customers, employees, advisors, and your gut. When the signals suggest that the path you are on is not going to take you where you want to go it is time to pivot.

So how do you pivot? Always be ready. Listen to your customers—they will tell you what they want. And when the time comes, pivot clearly and decisively. Understand what can be reused, what needs to be thrown away, and what else has to be built. Ensure that your team understands the pivot and is on board. Manage your cash and make sure your business partners, including your board, understand what you are doing and are supportive. Finally, assess whether you have the right skill sets for the new direction.

Every decision in the earliest days of your company is big. You are choosing north from south, but that cannot stop you from moving forward. Make decisions, always be assessing your situation, and expect to pivot as you find your way for your company.

---

*Google acquired Like.com as this book went to press.

THEME 5: FUNDRAISING

Most companies come to TechStars with a goal of raising money. One of the first things we do is make them take a step back and ask themselves "Do I need to raise money?" We're quite emphatic that the answer can be "No." Many great entrepreneurs are bootstrappers and huge companies have been created with little or no outside investment. And in every TechStars class to date, there has been at least one company that bootstrapped its way to success, such as J-Squared in 2007 and Occipital in 2008.

Of course, reality often knocks loudly. The vast majority of the startups that we work with will not be able to achieve profitability quickly enough to avoid death. So they look to investors—both angel and VC—to help them get their businesses up and running.

Entrepreneurs often fail to recognize that this is a major decision. When raising money from outside investors, there are always trade-offs. Before you raise money, the company is unambiguously your business. After you raise money, regardless of the amount, you now have new partners in your business. Investment usually comes with some level of board control and an expectation of larger returns. At the minimum, you have new people to share your ups and downs with.

Investors can be a great thing for a business. But they can also cause problems. Understanding the trade-offs, how to communicate and manage expectations, as well as what to expect is critical. Like any new relationship, the dynamics between you and your investors will likely be at a peak point the day after you close the investment. Your goal should be to develop and sustain a relationship over time with your investors. Even when your business hits the inevitable bumps in the road, you still need to have a healthy, constructive, and collaborative relationship with each other.

Some of the essays in this section are about the tactics of raising money but you'll see that a healthy dose of them relate to the alternatives. We think that you shouldn't start with the assumption that you need to raise money. And, if you do decide to raise money, make sure you know what you are getting yourself into.

You Don't Have to Raise Money

Joe Aigboboh and Jesse Tevelow

Joe and Jesse are the co-founders of J-Squared Media, a company that builds applications for social networks that are used by millions of end users. J-Squared completed TechStars in 2007 and quickly bootstrapped itself to profitability.

We entered the inaugural class of TechStars in 2007 with a simple concept for a content-sharing site. On the second day of the program, we decided to abandon our idea in search of a better business model. Within weeks, Facebook announced its platform and opened it to developers. While our business model was still unclear, we recognized the Facebook platform as a great opportunity to distribute products to a large and growing user base.

After about a week of experimenting, we launched our first app—Sticky Notes—that allowed users to send customized notes to their friends. The app grew to more than 10 million users in a matter of months, bringing in considerable revenues from banner advertising. By the time TechStars ended, we had funding offers from VCs as well as several acquisition offers. While most companies were seeking funding, we felt our early success had put us in a position to bootstrap our company.

The decision to bootstrap will affect many of your future operating decisions. We quickly realized that we needed to continue to drive revenue while controlling our costs. While this might have been obvious in hindsight, it caused us to focus on product decisions that resulted in a lot more revenue while operating under the constraints of very little cash. Our early revenue was composed primarily of advertising and sponsorships. We focused on growing revenues by searching for creative ways to increase traffic, optimizing our ads, and securing sponsorships.

With such a strong focus on maintaining profitability, we constantly evaluated the long-term feasibility of our revenue sources. As the online ad market soured, the constraints of self-funding forced us to identify viable long-term revenue sources immediately. We made a transition from advertising to virtual goods as a primary source of revenue faster than many well-funded competitors. Embracing the constraints of self-funding has allowed us to build a solid company with annual revenues of seven figures and growing.

Bootstrapping is not without its challenges. While it is often viewed from a financial perspective, it can also present challenges in other parts of the company. Some of our early hires sought the peace of mind offered by the backing of a VC despite our growing revenues and profitability. Fewer stakeholders means there are fewer people with a vested interest in helping you achieve your goals. For some, bootstrapping may also pose working capital challenges, making it difficult to grow quickly.

Despite the challenges, self-funding has allowed us to maintain complete control of our company as it has grown.

While we have avoided taking funding thus far, it doesn't mean we won't seek it eventually. However, should we decide to seek funding, we'll be able to negotiate better terms than if we had raised funding before defining our real business model or reaching profitability.

If there's one point to make about raising money, it's that there is no perfect formula. Defining your goals can help drive your decisions about funding. It's important to consider the advantages and challenges to self-funding, but remember that you don't necessarily have to raise money.

Joe and Jesse caught a wave at the very beginning of Facebook opening up their platform, and as a result, created a series of very popular Facebook applications early on. Given their visibility, they were approached by numerous investors and acquirers. In many cases, Joe and Jesse realized quickly that their long-term goals were not necessarily aligned with the investor or acquirer that had approached them. In other cases, the alignment was better, which resulted in deep and thoughtful conversations with their mentors. With every conversation, Joe and Jesse learned a lot—both about themselves as well as the opportunity they had in front of them. While making a decision about which path to go down was never easy, each situation challenged them and tested their commitment to the path they ultimately chose. Looking back on their progress over the past three years, it's clear that they chose the right path for themselves and their business.

There's More than One Way to Raise Money

Brad Feld

Brad is a managing director at Foundry Group and one of the co-founders of TechStars.

As a venture capitalist, I regularly hear the question "How do I raise money from a VC?" My response is usually "Why do you want to do that?"

Many entrepreneurs view raising money from a VC akin to finding the Holy Grail. Very few companies are VC-backed, however; most raise money from other sources, including friends and family, angels, customers, partners, and grants. Let's look at a few of these.

> *Friends and Family:* This is the most common form of a seed or early stage investment. Your first $10,000 will likely come from someone you know, like a parent, sibling, or co-worker. Sometimes this category is called the 3Fs (friends, family, and fools) mostly as a tongue-in-cheek way to signify how much of a risk

your early investors are taking. Recognize that they are betting on you, which is why they are often the first ones to invest.

Angel Investors: Angels come in many forms: the lone angel who is a successful entrepreneur who likes to invest in and get involved with startups; the super angel who invests in a large number of early stage companies; the newbie angel who has recently made some money and is looking to make some investments; or the angel group, which has a collection of angels that periodically invest together. Each category is different and as more organized angel groups have appeared, a wide variety of activities—some good and some bad—have emerged that connect entrepreneurs and angel investors. Many VC-backed companies get their first round from angel investors, which is a logical bridge to a VC round, especially for a first-time entrepreneur. But, be careful; for every angel investor, there is a corresponding devil investor.

Customers: The most satisfying form of early financing is revenue. My first company—Feld Technologies—raised just 10 dollars to get started. The balance of our investment came from our early customers. My partner and I started generating revenue shortly after we started the business, worked out of our apartments, and paid ourselves very little. At some point we were generating several thousand dollars per month of profit (not to be confused with positive cash flow, although we got there pretty quickly also) and we were able to bootstrap our company, never needing to raise any additional capital.

Partners: When you start your company, it's likely that you will collaborate with some other, more established companies. If you are working on something of value to them, they will often be willing to figure out a financial arrangement to help fund some of the work you are doing together. Don't be bashful about asking; if you don't ask, you'll never have a chance of getting something.

Grants: There have historically been a number of R&D programs backed by the U.S. government aimed at small businesses. The most notable is the Small Business Innovation Research (SBIR) program, which publishes a wide variety of technology research grants that startups can apply for. These grants are typically low margin, cost-plus type of arrangements, but the company gets to keep the intellectual property associated with the R&D. As a result, for R&D intensive companies, these can be good initial sources of financing.

Before you start thinking about raising money from venture capitalists, remember that there is more than one way to raise money to get your business started.

Brad Feld talks to the 2008 TechStars about raising money from angel investors.

Don't Forget about Bootstrapping

David Brown

David Brown is the president of ZOLL Medical Corporation. He is also one of the co-founders of TechStars, and has been a mentor since 2007.

When David Cohen and I started Pinpoint Technologies in 1993, I wish we had a program like TechStars. We had no mentors other than a former boss or two, we had no funding opportunities, and we didn't even know what an angel investor was. So we had to make it up as we went along and in many cases, reinvent the wheel.

One of the silver linings (at least with the benefit of my retrospectascope) is that without funding opportunities, we had to bootstrap our business. We had no money of our own, so we were forced to be extremely frugal. Armed with a few thousand dollars earned nights and weekends doing odd consulting work (including the glorious job of pulling cable and installing a network for a pest control company), we created a prototype and persuaded a prospective customer to lend us $100,000 in exchange for a free product and a repayment of the loan with interest. That product, without any additional investment, has now spawned a company with $40 million in annual sales and two hundred employees.

The value in bootstrapping wasn't so much that we retained 100 percent of the stock when we exited (although that was nice). More important to us was the ability to run the business as we saw fit, making the right decisions for us, for our customers, for our employees, and for the long-term benefit of the business. Conversely, so many companies raise money that then burns a hole in their pocket; they start hiring people, growing infrastructure, and in general spending way too much. Remember, investment is like a credit card; what you want in the long term is revenue. Revenue is justification that your customers want what you made; investment is just a one-time shot in the arm.

The most common argument for raising a large sum is to go faster: competitors are lurking around the corner, ready to launch at any second—we have to strike while the iron is hot! My experience is that this is rarely true. A good idea needs a little time to ferment and it needs to be fine-tuned to make sure it truly delights customers. Take the time to get it right and you'll find that those competitors might not be as close as you think.

Bootstrapping, of course, isn't always possible. Sometimes startup costs such as inventory, development work, or infrastructure require some investment. In fact, I take the liberty of defining *bootstrapping* as raising the least amount of money needed to get a business off the ground. Taking this approach makes sure that you right-size your business, not letting your expenses get ahead of your revenues. After all, you wouldn't want to pay your rent by credit card, would you?

David Cohen and David Brown founded Pinpoint Technologies together in 1993. They were bootstrappers from the start. They had hired a great programmer named Eran Shay early on. Rather than buying a second computer (Pentium-90s were expensive at the time!) David and Eran worked in 12-hour shifts so that they could share the one fast machine that they owned. David worked from 9 A.M. to 9 P.M. most days, and Eran worked from 9 P.M. to 9 A.M. It was only when they got their first paying customer that they splurged for a second computer.

Beware of Angel Investors Who Aren't

David Cohen

David is a co-founder and the CEO of TechStars.

I have been involved in several angel groups, and most of them have sucked. The reason is very simple—most of the members of most angel groups are not actually angel investors. They're often there for what I call *gig-flow*. They're looking for startups that they can jump on board with, either as an employee or consultant. Or they are there to meet rich people, drink wine, and eat tiny sandwiches. Finally, they're often there to preside over cute little startups that ask them for money. As a special bonus, they get to have a good laugh afterward.

Do I sound jaded? I draw on direct experience. When I first started angel investing, I quite naturally joined the local angel group in my city. I'd estimate that 95 percent of the members of the group had done at most one angel investment in their entire lives and many had never done any. I quickly figured out that I could generate much more interesting deal flow by getting to know other real angel investors and by creating my own independent brand and visibility. It turns out that strong entrepreneurs are pretty good at finding people who actually make angel investments. And it seems to me that people who don't actually make angel investments, but tell the world they do, aren't really serious about it.

Adverse selection was plainly evident to me in the angel group meetings I attended because the companies that were pitching typically had been unsuccessful at raising money from committed and professional angel investors. While there were a few exceptions, these companies already had some momentum with their financings and were looking for a few more investors to help them finish up their round.

After talking to a number of other active angel investors, I determined that while there were a few excellent angel groups, most of them were full of fake angel investors. These fake angels are unlikely to fund your company. There's also a second class of angel investors who really aren't. They are the unscrupulous types that often use egregious tactics and terms.

One example that I seem to encounter over and over again is the bait-and-switch angel investor. He's usually got an interesting background and it seems like he might have a pile of cash to invest. The story goes something like this. He offers to put together a half-million dollar round for you. He's committing a hundred thousand dollars! So far, so good. However, once the round starts coming together, he starts backing off his personal investment (usually all the way down to zero) and instead rides the momentum into a job. Instead of investing, he'll become the CEO or chairman, and will take a bunch of equity to boot. Unbeknownst to you, this supposed angel investor is running this same game with as many interesting (and struggling!) startups as he can until he finds one that people actually want to invest in. Bingo—the bait-and-switch angel investor just landed a year or two of guaranteed salary and a bunch of equity on the backs of bright young entrepreneurs overly desperate to raise a round.

Then there's the term driver. This type of angel investor is going to drive a hard bargain. They're going to put in $50,000 and spark the round for you. They just ultimately want about 75 percent of the company to do it. They simply don't get it and are hunting for suckers. You're not a sucker, but you're still going to spend months with this person if you're not careful. The cost to you is going to be measured in time.

There are a handful of very straightforward tactics to making sure you're dealing with a legitimate angel investor. First, ask the prospective investor how long he has been making angel investments, how many he has made, and how much he typically invests each time. If you get dodgy answers, or fundamentally tiny ones such as "I've done one angel investment in the last seventeen years," beware. Don't proceed with any other questions until you have this answer.

If an angel investor says he is just getting into making angel investments, this should set off your Spidey sense. In this case, do your homework and start checking highly trusted references that you source yourself. Check with known reputable angel investors and local venture capitalists on both the person and the companies he has been involved in to get a sense of how real the prospective investor is. Research his background—is he really likely to have the type of money necessary to make angel investments?

If your prospective investor says he's been investing for a year or more, ask him to introduce you to two companies he has invested in during the last year. If he can't name two in the past year, then ask him for the last three he has invested in. If there aren't three, recognize that this person is at best investing as a hobbyist and has very limited experience doing so. Now call or e-mail all three companies and ask to speak to the founders. Verify that the person actually invested dollars in that company. Check the reference while you're at it and ask if they were helpful to the company or not.

None of these questions or tactics will be offensive to real angel investors. In fact, they will give the real ones more confidence in you. These tactics might offend the fake ones, driving them away. Recognize that that's just fine.

Beware of angel investors who aren't. They'll put you through endless diligence, play bait-and-switch with your financing, and generally waste your time.

David's crappy experiences with several angel groups led him to check out an event in Los Angeles that Jason Calacanis put together called the Open Angel Forum. It was a zero-pretense event with five high quality companies having dinner with 15 to 20 super angels (those who have made at least four notable investments in the past 12 months). It's free to entrepreneurs, which was the key attractor for David. He loved it so much that he started the second chapter in Colorado. Now the Open Angel Forum is spreading all over the world. Check it out at openangelforum.com.

David Cohen explaining something that he's obviously emphatic about.

Seed Investors Care about Three Things

Jeff Clavier

Jeff is a seed investor through his fund SoftTech VC. He has been a TechStars mentor since 2007.

In August 2010, my family celebrated the 10-year anniversary of our move from France to Silicon Valley as well as my joining the venture capital industry. Six of these 10 years will have been spent working with very early stage teams, ranging from the raw idea stage to the point at which the initial product worked so well that the company has two founders and tens of millions of avid users.

One of the most common questions I get several times a week is "What characteristics are you looking for in an early stage company before making an investment?" You could list 10 criteria, 20 things, or 30 checklist items and they would all be valid—things like the result of lessons learned, experience gained, and mistakes made. In the investing business, you can only learn the hard way—by losing or by wasting money on things that eventually don't work.

Seed investors—people like me who are typically putting the first chunk of cash into a new startup—have the shortest checklist. Because we invest so early in the life of a company, a lot of the data points that later-stage investors are using to evaluate an opportunity are not yet available to us. So I focus on three things: "People, Products, and Markets." Or actually:

People Products and Markets

First of all, the market the entrepreneurs are going after needs to be "big enough." You will often hear VCs state that an opportunity is "too small for them," that they don't see "VC-type returns," or can't see a "$1 billion company." When you are investing very early, you want to make sure that the target market feels big enough; that is, that the company you are looking at investing in can reasonably grow revenues to $10 million or more in three years and $50-to-$100 million in five to seven years without needing 100 percent adoption.

Next, I look for products that win users over. You either have users (alpha, beta, gamma, whatever you call them doesn't matter) or you don't. If you don't, I'll look at mockups and demos to figure out if what you are building will get the traction that you are claiming it will. But it is tough to figure this out since having users is real external validation that your product is perceived as interesting, valuable, and differentiated and one day, maybe, someone would actually pay for it. As a former product guy, I will also spend a lot of time using the product myself, trying to assess some of the characteristics I just mentioned.

But, most importantly, it's all about the *Peeps*. Until recently, my trifecta "People, Products, Markets" used to be "People, People, People" but I adjusted it because the product and market clearly have impact on my early stage investment decisions. I'm looking for a variety of characteristics in early stage entrepreneurs, such as:

- Passion
- Determination, dedication, and tenacity
- Raw intelligence
- Agility and resourcefulness

- Clarity and focus
- Empathy
- Natural leadership
- Working smart rather than working hard (okay, working hard, too)
- Team dynamics

All these characteristics are important. While some are more important than others, founding teams display different mixes of these. Think of them as being weights of different shapes and sizes that you place on a scale: at some point the scale will tip—and you will get a funding offer (or not). In recent years, where capital efficiency has been a prevalent factor in building an entire generation of consumer Internet companies, the traits I favor the most are determination, agility, clarity, and working smart.

I've recently started using the following tag line for my firm SoftTech VC:

> Seeking the perfect combo: "a smart-ass team with a kick-ass product in a big-ass market."

I think that it perfectly embodies what I am doing for a living, and it's easily shortened to "The Three Asses Rule" once you know the long version.

Jeff has been involved in TechStars from the very beginning. He flies out to Boulder midway through the program every year, spends an entire day at TechStars, and visits with each team. Jeff uses this to play a dual purpose—he's acting as a mentor to help shape and focus the teams and he's also efficiently evaluating 10 prospective investments. Having watched Jeff over the years, he leaves Boulder pretty sure which of the teams he's interested in investing in and then quickly makes a decision after investor day. Now that's the kind of seed investor a first-time entrepreneur is looking for!

Jeff Clavier looking for the perfect "Three Ass" company at TechStars in 2009.

Practice Like You Play

Alex White

Alex is founder and CEO of Next Big Sound, a company that provides online music analytics and insights, which raised about $1 million from Foundry Group, Alsop-Louie Partners, and SoftTech VC after completing TechStars in 2009.

Raising money from investors was unlike anything else I'd ever done in my life. When I tried my hardest in school, previous jobs, and extracurricular activities, I had a sense that if I exceeded some threshold I'd be able to get the A, promotion, or leadership position I wanted. When raising the first round of financing for my company, I could give the best presentation in the world, but if the investor was uncomfortable with any part of the team, idea, revenue model, competition, industry, market size, amount of money we were asking for, our development time line, how it fit with their portfolio companies, or an almost infinite list of other variables, then the funding wouldn't happen.

With so many factors at play, there are numerous issues that can derail a financing. The trick is to present a compelling solution to a big problem and then have the right answers to every conceivable question the potential investor might ask. For me, the first part is the easy one since most entrepreneurs wouldn't be pouring their hearts into a business if they didn't think they had a great answer to a big problem. The trouble comes when the investor begins to pry into any number of factors looking for any reason whatsoever why the deal is not a strong investment. By virtue of being a startup, there will be uncertainties and reasons not to put money on the line. Investors just need to know you are aware of the unknowns and understand how you are systematically addressing them.

People do not like being separated from their money. If you've ever tried charging customers for a product or service, you have some idea about the tangible value you need to provide for them to justify a purchase. Now imagine trying to persuade them to write you a check but instead of trading their hard-earned dollars in exchange for something immediate, you just promise that you'll deliver it in the future, and the way they will experience it will be indirectly through the increase in the value of their investment in your company.

So, to be successful at fundraising, I practiced like crazy. I must have rewritten our pitch 100 times and practiced it 500 times. The benefit of running it past dozens of people for feedback was invaluable because it's nearly impossible to separate yourself from the day-to-day business long enough to put together a high-level pitch that makes any sense. By the time we got to TechStars Demo Day I had well-rehearsed answers to every question I was asked. While the experience of fundraising was totally new to me, I had to remember that many of the investors had been hearing pitches, scheduling follow-up meetings, and grilling entrepreneurs since before I was even born. The investors had years of experience and I could tell they were mapping my business, my answers, and my confidence to all their previous successes and failures, trying to draw out the patterns to identify if we were a winner. All we had was our passion, incredible team, strong presentation, insane optimism, and confidence from a full summer of practice.

Fundraising is a full-time job and it requires the full attention of at least one team member and the cooperation of the rest of the team to prepare the presentation, hear the pitch over and over, and help brainstorm potential questions and the right answers to those questions. People want to invest in winners. Winners are confident, and confidence comes from practicing like you play. This means pitching in front of people, getting grilled by colleagues, mentors, and friends, and explaining your business until answering the question of how you're going to make money is so boring it makes you sick. How are you going to get someone to write you a check if you can't confidently describe what they will get in return?

Alex isn't exaggerating when he says he must have practiced his presentation 500 times. When he gave it on TechStars Demo Day in front of a packed room of investors, he nailed it. If judges were handing out scores, he would have gotten a perfect 10 from each of them.

This paid huge dividends for Next Big Sound. The clarity of Alex's presentation combined with the progress that Next Big Sound made during TechStars resulted in a huge interest in their angel round. Alex and his partners decided they were going to raise only a modest amount of money and had commitments of at least three times what they wanted to raise. They had to make difficult decisions about which investors to take but they did this gracefully.

There's a well-known cliché popularized by Malcolm Gladwell that to be great at something you have to invest 10,000 hours in it. While you might not have to practice your pitch for 10,000 hours, you should practice it enough times so that you can give it from beginning to end with your eyes closed in a noisy bar when your friends are throwing things at you. When you are comfortable in that environment, you are ready to roll.

Alex White of Next Big Sound played like he practiced at Demo Day, Summer 2009.

If You Want Money, Ask for Advice

Nicole Glaros

Nicole is the general manager of TechStars in Boulder.

TechStars founders who are adept at actively engaging mentors and investors early in the program (and consequentially *before* fundraising) seem to have more success raising external capital later compared to founders who struggle to solicit and embrace mentorship. Why?

When you want advice, ask for money. When you want money, ask for advice. I believe there are three reasons this adage holds true.

Investors say no more than they say yes. An investor is constantly being bombarded by requests for capital. It's fundamental to his job. Statistics vary, but it wouldn't be unusual for an investor to say yes less than 1 percent of the time. Given that there are only two answers to the question "Will you invest?" they become adept at quickly discovering weaknesses and saying no. When approached, they are wearing their investor hat and their senses instinctively hone in on the negatives of the company. Most investors don't want to turn you away empty-handed, though, so they will offer advice for overcoming any weaknesses.

Risk mitigation. Getting investors and mentors involved early in your company before you start raising capital provides them a way to track your progress and learn about you before any risk is taken. Asking for guidance here doesn't have to be a yes or no question. You can ask for open-ended advice, such as "Which business model might work better in this market?" Many are willing to put in time and mentorship to get you to a point at which you are a lower risk than another investment opportunity. Also, engaging them early gets them excited about your company and you, not just in the investment, so initially they will be focused more on the business instead of the returns.

What someone helps write, they will help underwrite. Once you begin soliciting and following the advice of mentors and investors, they are more likely to be actively engaged with you and the business. Once they see they can have a direct impact on your decisions and the directions of the company, they'll begin to feel a sense of ownership in the outcomes. And once they have that sense of ownership, they will go to lengths to help you get to the next level. Whether it's through introductions, endorsements, fundraising, or just spending more time, they will help underwrite your business if they feel like they've had a part in creating it.

If you're looking to raise capital later, engage great mentors and investors from the beginning, before you start fundraising. Seek their advice and guidance early on. Learn when to take their advice, but be sure that you communicate the reasons why some guidance wasn't followed. Let them and their experience help shape the company, the vision, the direction, the product, and the execution. Make them an active part of your team, let them see the progress you've made, and get them excited about what you're doing. When it comes time to raise capital, you'll have a champion on your side who is more likely to open the checkbook and encourage others to do the same.

At TechStars, many investors are involved throughout the program as mentors. These investors realize they are playing the role of mentor, and we encourage the companies not to view them as fresh meat but rather as early advisors. By using these investors as advisors, the entrepreneurs develop a real relationship with these potential investors. It usually becomes clear over time whether the investor is going to be interested in participating in a financing. If she is, that's great, but even if she isn't, the entrepreneurs have benefited from the interaction.

Nicole provides feedback to the teams and is recorded by Megan Sweeney, who produces "The Founders" web video series.

Show, Don't Tell

Brad Feld

Brad is a managing director at Foundry Group and one of the co-founders of TechStars.

I get e-mails every day from folks either raising money or telling me about their new idea and asking for feedback. The conventional wisdom is that VCs rarely invest in things that reach them randomly (or *over the transom* in someone's VC vocabulary—I can't for the life of me figure out why that phrase hangs around.) However, this isn't the case for Foundry Group, as several of the companies we've funded in the past two years were initially from cold call e-mail inquiries (Brightleaf and Organic Motion). I'm very happy to get a steady stream of random e-mails—keep them coming!

I've noticed a trend toward more video presentations lately and I'm reminded of the old writer's adage "Show, don't tell." This applies nicely to every pitch you ever do. Specifically, I don't want to hear you describe what you are going to do; I want to see it. If you haven't built it yet, show me an example. It's always better to point me at a

URL, even if it's a very rough prototype, as I can usually get a much quicker view of what you are doing by simply playing around.

One video I watched recently was a two-minute segment of the entrepreneur looking into the camera and describing his business idea. The idea was fine although I could tell within 15 seconds that it wasn't something we'd invest in given the market he was going after. I ended up watching the full two-minute video to see if he ever shifted from "tell" mode to "show" mode. He never did—the two minutes ended and the whole video was the entrepreneur describing his idea.

This was a wasted opportunity by the entrepreneur in my book. I could have read one paragraph that contained the same content. The entrepreneur didn't take advantage of the medium (video) in any way. While he did a nice job on the monologue, he wasn't trying out for a TV commercial, a TV show, or a movie. He missed the goal of getting my attention and hopefully getting me to engage with him at the next level.

For most of the great VCs I know, the way an entrepreneur makes a connection when there is no pre-existing relationship is to generate an immediate interest with the product. That's what happened for us in the case of Brightleaf and Organic Motion. The entrepreneurs were highly credible, but more importantly we immediately got excited about their products, which caused us to be more interested in going deep and exploring an investment.

This is a repeating theme that for some reason isn't said strongly enough. The great entrepreneurs (and salespeople) show. Just think of how Steve Jobs does it. Show me!

Turn the Knife after You Stick It in

David Cohen

David is a co-founder and the CEO of TechStars.

At TechStars, we've worked hard to teach entrepreneurs how to "turn the knife." Whether you're presenting your company to investors, partners, or customers you should focus on the pain you address before you discuss the tremendous solution you're bringing to the market.

Describing the pain is usually quite natural, but many people forget to finish the job. Think of describing the pain as sticking the knife in. Your job is not done. You have to really make me feel it. You do this by twisting the knife slowly, deliberately, and repeatedly.

SendGrid, one of the TechStars Boulder 2009 companies, does an excellent job of turning the knife. Their product improves the deliverability, scalability, accountability, and reliability of software-generated e-mail. Sounds like a real problem, right? The following is how they turn the knife.

"Twenty percent of legitimate e-mails sent by software companies to their customers will end up in spam folders."

Ouch.

"A large e-commerce company determined that if just 1 percent of their annual e-mail notifications aren't delivered, it costs them fourteen million dollars in lost sales."

Stop it!

"This same company figured out that at least 7 percent of their e-mail is ending up being marked as spam. This problem is literally costing them a hundred million dollars a year."

I'm begging you—show mercy!

"This is an epidemic with a staggering financial cost. There are thousands of companies right now that can't deliver legitimate e-mail to their own customers."

You're killing me here!

Twisting the knife is key, but make sure you stop and shift to talking about the solution just before you kill them, but not much earlier. Don't just show them the pain; make them beg for it to stop before moving on.

SendGrid went on to turn the knife on Demo Day using some of these very statements, and ultimately went on to raise nearly $6 million in venture capital. They made the investors feel the pain, and then showed them an elegant solution. Billions of e-mails later, SendGrid is a real painkiller.

David Cohen twisting the knife against a feeble opponent during the second annual Ben Casnocha TechStars Table Tennis Invitational Tournament.

Don't Overoptimize on Valuations

Kirk Holland

Kirk is a general partner at Vista Ventures, an early stage venture capital firm, and has been a TechStars mentor since 2008.

Since I'm an early stage investor, I'm biased, but I think it's very important to make sure that your early investors are rewarded if your company is successful.

Companies going through the TechStars program have historically had pre-money valuations after the program in the $1.5 million to $4 million range. However, these early stage companies are not really worth millions of dollars when they finish the TechStars program and we make a deliberate point of reminding them of this. Forget what the market is. When someone invests a million dollars in a company at a very early stage they often wouldn't be off-base asking for half or even two-thirds of your company.

It often takes entrepreneurs a few moments of honest reflection before they realize this simple truth. Stop and think about it for a second: Someone is putting one million dollars into a startup that most likely has almost no revenue and is by definition extremely risky. Most startups fail and in this case they're going to be out a million bucks! What if that was your million dollars and this was somebody else's baby?

However, the best early stage investors ask for somewhere between 20 and 33 percent of the company for that kind of money. This is because they recognize two very important facts. First, the entrepreneurs need to retain a big chunk of the company in order to stay motivated and eventually reap the rewards of their hard work over time. Second, the company is probably going to have to raise more money and it's going to create more dilution for the entrepreneurs.

In terms of valuation, TechStars has had a couple of outliers on the high end and in those cases the companies predictably ended up limiting their options. For investors and founders to be happy, valuations must go up at a reasonable rate over time. We all hope that new investors in a future round will value the company higher because it will have demonstrated value and simply be worth more. If you raise your first round on a $10 million pre-money valuation, you've got a very long way to go to make it worth $15 million or $20 million for the next round. But if you raise your first round on a $2.5 million pre-money valuation, getting to $5 million in value is much more attainable. If your first round was priced too high you can't demonstrate that kind of growth in value, you're not going to have happy investors, or there's going to be a serious hit on the founder's equity. Each of these things can end up severely limiting your options.

Recognize the risk that your early investors are taking. They're jumping into the trenches with you, betting on you and your team, and risking their capital and their reputation, too. By accepting a low (also known as "more than fair") valuation, you recognize the risk that they take and you ensure a meaningful reward when you're successful. As a bonus, your investors are going to want to back you again and again because you're a true partner who optimizes not only for yourself but for all of your stakeholders.

It's important to realize that not all investors are equal. In many cases, a great investor who can help your company is worth much more than an unknown investor who will give you money and then disappear, or worse, torture you with inane questions. In addition to not overoptimizing on valuation, you should work hard to get the highest quality and most capable investors into your company, even if that means trading off a somewhat lower valuation. Remember, you'll be living with your investors for a long time—choose wisely.

Get Help with Your Term Sheet

Jason Mendelson

Jason is a managing director at Foundry Group and has been a TechStars mentors since 2007.

The good news is that you received a term sheet from an investor wanting to give you a much-needed financing. The bad news is now you have try to understand what all this legal jargon means and how to negotiate for the best possible deal. So how do you do it?

First, realize that you'll never be as good at negotiating a term sheet as an investor who regularly invests in startups. And you'll also never be as good as his lawyer. So as a first step, make sure that you have good legal counsel.

But that doesn't mean that you should just send your lawyer the term sheet and say, "Finish it." There are too many important issues to deal with and you need to have a working knowledge of what the terms mean, which ones matter, and what some of the trade-offs are that your business will make should you accept certain provisions.

In general, there are only two things that investors really care about when making investments: returns and control. *Returns* refers to the end-of-the-day financial return the investor will get and the terms that have direct impact on these economics. *Control* refers to mechanisms that allow the investors to either affirmatively exercise control over the business or to veto certain decisions the company can make. If you are negotiating a deal and an investor is digging his heels in on a provision that doesn't affect the returns or control, they are probably blowing smoke, rather than elucidating substance. Or perhaps they aren't that sophisticated or, worse, are just jerks.

You should focus on terms like *pre-money valuation, liquidation preferences, board of director elections, drag-along rights,* and *protective provisions.* Most of the other terms you'll see in a standard term sheet aren't really all that important. If the person you are negotiating with thinks they are, this is important information for you to know before entering into a business partnership with him.

Many of these terms have interdependencies and it's important that you understand how terms such as *option pools, warrant grants,* and *the election of independent board members* will affect returns and control. For example, what might look like a great pre-money valuation might not be if the investor is demanding a larger option pool or grant of a warrant—each of which dilute your ownership.

When you do sit down to negotiate, be honest and forthright. If you are dealing with a reputable investor, talking about the trade-offs and issues usually allows the parties to become more comfortable with each other and work better later as partners. These negotiations often forge the future relationship of the entrepreneur and investor.

For detailed information on important terms such as *pre-money valuation, liquidation preference, board of director elections, drag-along rights,* and *protective provisions,* see the extensive term sheet series of blog posts written by Jason and Brad at Feld.com.

Jason Mendelson participating in a session at TechStars in 2007.

Focus on the First One-Third

Brad Feld

Brad is a managing director at Foundry Group and one of the co-founders of TechStars.

Raising money from angel investors can be a daunting task. One useful mental trick that we teach founders at TechStars is to focus on getting the first one-third of the money committed. If you've gotten a third of the round committed, you'll often find that the rest of the financing will come together quickly. The reason is that angel investing is best understood as a social sport. If you've got one-third, you have a lead investor, or at least a lead group of investors.

Generally speaking, you are going to encounter three types of angel investors. The first type is the potential leads. They're not going to play wait and see. They'll lead the round if they get excited about it. This is generally the same class of angel investor who will also say no quickly. Recognize that this is great in either case. At least you'll know where you stand with this type of angel investor. Generally, focusing on the first one-third means focusing on this first type of angel investor.

The second type of investor (and they're very common) is the kind that will not commit early on, but will want you to keep them in the loop. These are the maybes. These are great to collect, but I've seen too many entrepreneurs spend all their time trying to convert maybes into lead investors. My advice is simply to collect the maybes, ask them if you can tell others that they're interested, keep them posted on your progress, and get back to identifying more people who have the potential to lead.

Recognize that the same angel investor will behave differently in different deals, so it's dangerous to stereotype any particular prospective angel investor into one of these first two categories.

The third type of angel investor is the most dangerous. They're the angel investors who aren't really angel investors. You may mistake them for the first type, and they'll ultimately cause massive distraction and delay. See "Beware of Angel Investors Who Aren't" for more on this.

Mentally segment every angel investor you meet into one of these three buckets as quickly as possible. Then focus on the first type and imagine them making up one-third of the funding pie. Once you're there, push aggressively toward the closing with the goal of moving the *maybe* group into the *yes* or *no* group. You'll need to set a closing date that the lead group is happy with or you won't have any leverage to move the second type of investor off the fence.

Usually the second and third pieces of the pie will come together much more quickly. The committed angels will start calling their friends to get the deal done, and some of the maybes will fill in the gap.

It doesn't always work this way of course, but there does seem to be something magical about focusing on the first third of the pie.

THEME 6: LEGAL AND STRUCTURE

While team issues are one of the top startup killers, things left undocumented also often lead to fatal problems later. Too many founders ignore legal and structural issues, assuming they can deal with them later. Sometimes they're right. Sometimes they're dead.

Within TechStars, we have active early engagement from several startup lawyers, accountants, and bankers. These firms provide free advice early in the program and make sure the companies get formed correctly. Most entrepreneurial law firms, accounting firms, and banks will do the same for your company, if you ask. In addition to being good business development activities for them because they'd love you to be their customer as you grow your business, it's also an important and effective way for them to engage in the entrepreneurial ecosystem.

Now, we'd never recommend that you go overboard on the legal and structure issues. There are simple and cost-effective ways to do things right. Taking the time now to understand the most important issues can save your startup (and you) a great deal of pain down the road.

Form the Company Early

Brad Bernthal

Brad is an associate clinical professor at the University of Colorado Law School and the director of entrepreneurial initiatives at Silicon Flatirons. He has been a TechStars mentor since 2008.

Many entrepreneurs are surprised to learn that a business is already a legal entity—at least, technically—even if they did not take action to legally form the company. This is like thinking you're not going to the prom only to find out that your parents have already arranged the date.

Like a prom date arranged by your parents, the default entity for your business is probably not the one that you want to dance with, let alone get married to. The following are three key drivers to guide when and why you need to select a legal entity that fits your business.

First, limit personal exposure. Ask yourself—if something goes awry, could this business create liabilities that should be separate from me as an individual? An operating business is, by default, a sole proprietorship (if operated by one person) or a general partnership (more than one person). Here's the problem: these legal forms do not separate a business's liabilities from a person's individual liabilities.

As a result, an owner in a default entity is personally liable for the business's problems. For example, your partner signs the business up for a year-long lease. The startup fails. Guess who might be on the hook to pay the rent owed for the remainder of the lease? You (and your partner). It is time to get protection if your startup is ready to enter into contracts, release a product, or take on debts. Proper formation of an appropriate legal entity for a startup (typically, a limited liability corporation [LLC], an S-Corp, or a C-Corp) separates a business's liabilities from a person's individual liability. Formation is not unduly complicated and your company is not married to a certain form forever. For example, the conversion from something like an LLC to a C-Corp is relatively straightforward.

Second, lock down your intellectual property (IP). Make sure you do not inadvertently leave critical IP outside the company. If you are involved in a technology startup and the crown jewels of your company relate to its IP, you want to protect it! It sounds easy, but following this advice is not always intuitive. For example, roughly over half of the companies that come to the Colorado Law School's Entrepreneurial Law Clinic previously worked with independent contractors on a handshake basis. These companies are surprised to learn that the contractor, not the company, may well own IP developed by the contractor. A simple solution when working with independent contractors is to have a written contract that unambiguously assigns IP over to the company. By having a legal entity formed, it is easier to have agreements and assignments that get IP into the company.

Third, decide who owns what. When you organize a company, sort out the ownership among the founders. Ownership disputes are a startup killer. Ownership matters can be delicate discussions, of course; however, it is always easier to address ownership before the business succeeds, instead of after there is real money to fight over. Moreover, if founders cannot navigate ownership discussions early on, this is likely a red flag of communication failures to come.

A classic problem following a failure to address ownership is the wayward founder. Imagine a team of four friends who work on a product but never organize an entity or talk about ownership shares. Six months in, one team member moves on in life (graduates, gets married and moves away, or takes a "real" job). The three remaining team members keep going. Two years later, the company starts to click. Guess who inevitably learns of the company's success, thinks his contribution was the most important part of the business, and returns to claim 25 percent ownership of the company? Yep, old friend Number 4. Forming the company and explicitly determining ownership prevents the wayward founder problem.

A great resource for first-time entrepreneurs is their local university. Most schools have at least one professor who is focused on entrepreneurship; many have entire departments and programs. But don't limit yourself to just the business school. As Brad and his team at Silicon Flatirons have demonstrated, the law school can often be a source of entrepreneurial education. Furthermore, most of the actual innovation is happening in other departments, such as engineering, computer science, and the life sciences.

While advice and opportunities around entrepreneurship are available from universities, the real power develops when the university engages in the local entrepreneurial community. The stories of entrepreneurship surrounding MIT and Stanford are well known, but this isn't limited to the top-tier schools. The University of Colorado at Boulder—especially Silicon Flatirons—has done a brilliant job of engaging with TechStars, including them in the Entrepreneurial Law Clinic, hosting them at the New Tech Meetups that occur at the CU Law Wolf Building, and getting them involved in the Entrepreneurs Unplugged Series that Brad Feld co-hosts with Brad Bernthal.

Don't overlook the power of your university and it's engagement in your entrepreneurial community, especially early in the life of your company.

Choose the Right Company Structure

Brad Feld

Brad is a managing director at Foundry Group and one of the co-founders of TechStars.

Photo by Scott Cejka

When you start your company, you need to choose the type of corporate form you want. There are two logical choices (S-Corp or C-Corp), and a third one (LLC) that pops up occasionally. The best choice depends on the financing path you are ultimately planning on going down.

   S-Corp: If you are not going to raise any VC or angel money, an S-Corp is the best structure because it has all the tax benefits and flexibility of a partnership—specifically, a single tax structure versus the potential for double tax structure of a C-Corp—while retaining the liability protection of a C-Corp.

   C-Corp: If you are going to raise VC or angel money, a C-Corp is the best (and often required) structure. In a VC or angel-backed company, you'll almost always end up with multiple classes of stock, which are not permitted in an S-Corp. Since a VC or angel-backed company is expected to lose money for a while (that's why you are taking the investment in the first place!) the double-taxation issues will be deferred for a while, plus it's unlikely you'll be distributing money out of a VC or angel-backed company when you become profitable.

LLC: An LLC (limited liability corporation) will often substitute for an S-Corp (it has similar dynamics), although it's much harder to effectively grant equity (membership units in the case of an LLC versus options in an S-Corp or C-Corp—most employees understand and have had experience with options, but many don't understand membership units). LLCs work really well for companies with a limited number of owners and not so well when the ownership starts to be spread among multiple people.

While there are several advantages of an LLC over an S-Corp (the ability to issue different classes of securities, ease of set-up, informality of operating agreements, lower state taxes, non-U.S. investors), venture funds typically cannot (or don't want to) invest in LLCs. When a VC invests in an LLC, she risks getting assessed an income tax called UBTI (unrelated business tax income). Investors in venture fund partnerships frown upon this type of income and most funds have a provision in their fund agreements that they will use best efforts not to bring UBTI into the partnership. As a result, VC funds shy away from investing in LLCs.

The able-minded entrepreneur says, "Yeah, but I'm not ready for venture capital yet. I'll just do an LLC now and convert to a C-Corp when I raise VC in a year." Okay, but to convert an LLC into a C-Corp, one actually has to go through a complete merger, whereby a new entity is created, which usually devolves into a wholly owned subsidiary, and that subsidiary is merged into the LLC, leaving the LLC as the subsidiary of the parent. In short, it's complicated and makes the lawyers and accountants some extra cash. Yuck.

In contrast, converting an S-Corp to a C-Corp is simply a "check the box" tax election (or—actually—unchecking the box). This can be done in a day with a single tax form. No lawyers, no accountants, no expense. Therefore, while the LLC has some benefits, the costs of converting the LLC into a fundable entity are substantially higher and usually not worth the additional effort.

An established lawyer who does corporate work with early stage or VC-backed companies can set this up quickly, easily, and inexpensively for you. Such a lawyer is often the best source for the equivalent of a best practices template, since this is routine work and requires simple boilerplate documents and filings.

Default to Delaware

Jon Taylor

Jon is a partner at Kendall, Koenig, and Oelsner, PC. He has been a TechStars mentor since 2008.

You've worked for months toward closing your seed financing. From initial pitches, term sheets, due diligence, and definitive documents, you have finally reached the finish line and are scheduled to close on the day before Thanksgiving except for one significant problem. Your counsel informs you that despite paying a $700 fee for same-day service, the company's amended and restated articles of incorporation will not be filed in time to close because the secretary of state of California has rejected them. It seems a staff lawyer at the secretary of state's office has determined that a requirement in the articles that certain actions be approved by "a majority of the board, including the preferred directors" is in conflict with California law. Despite a history of both company and investor counsel having included this provision in many past filings and the fact that there is no specific provision of the California code prohibiting such a provision, the filing will not be made in time and the closing will need to be pushed back for at least another five days. This kind of thing happens frequently in California. It doesn't happen in Delaware.

While avoiding the capriciousness of the staff lawyers employed by the secretary of state of California is one reason for incorporating your company in Delaware, it is not the primary reason. Delaware corporate law is generally considered pro-company. This not only means that Delaware provides shareholders flexibility in creating specific terms for corporate governance and has systems in place for quick and painless corporate filings, but, more importantly, it means that Delaware provides management and directors with guidelines based on a well-developed body of corporate law as to how to comply with their fiduciary duties in a number of different situations. In short, Delaware law provides founders, investors, and directors with certainty and uniformity regarding their relationship to the company and its stakeholders.

Corporate law is generally a matter of state law. Each state is free to develop its own rules and regulations regarding how a company is formed and operated and the fiduciary duties of the board of directors, management, and majority stockholders. This has the potential to create uncertainty for investors that need to have clear guidelines regarding the legal structure of their investments in many different states and their fiduciary duties as board members. Thus, investors will overwhelmingly encourage or require their portfolio companies to incorporate in Delaware. Delaware case law provides clear guidelines as to how directors should act in certain situations. Over the last 90 years or so, Delaware courts have refined concepts such as the business-judgment rule regarding decisions made by the board of directors, as well as the Revlon and Unocal tests regarding the fiduciary duties of the board in connection with a sale of a company. For the most part, Delaware courts have recognized the inherent riskiness of business and don't attempt to second-guess the decisions of the board of directors. For example, under the business judgment rule, Delaware courts will presume that the actions of a director are "on an informed basis, in good faith and in the honest belief that the action taken was in the best interests of the company," and will not review such actions except in very specific circumstances.

Other states do not have this body of case law to help guide directors in making decisions on behalf of the company, which creates uncertainty regarding the appropriate actions that need to be taken for directors to comply with their fiduciary duties. Although corporate attorneys may assume that a particular state court will follow Delaware's guidance on an issue, such courts have no obligation to do so. This uncertainty can be avoided simply by incorporating in Delaware.

Jon's advice may seem overly lawyerly, but it's really important. We've been in many bizarre situations because companies incorporated in different states. California law is different from Texas law, which is different from Illinois law, which is different from Massachusetts law, and so on until you count to 50. Many lawyers don't know the corporate laws of states other than their own, or worse, think they do and then immediately get you into trouble because they really don't. Keep it simple—incorporate in Delaware.

Lawyers Don't Have to Be Expensive

Michael Platt

Michael is a partner at Cooley LLP and has been a TechStars mentor since 2007.

> *Lawyers are too expensive. We're a stealthy, scrappy startup. We are just going to use the family lawyer or, better yet, file an LLC certificate ourselves. When we get the prototype finished and we get a VC term sheet, we can fix whatever we mess up. Let's just initial the page with our equity splits so there is no dispute later.*
>
> —The Thrifty Entrepreneur

That's a great example of the application of the 80/20 rule, and 80 percent of the time it's the most cost-effective answer. But 20 percent of the time something different from what you anticipate occurs. It's different because you haven't had the opportunity to see 300 start-ups in formation and financing. For example, take the example I have seen a half-dozen times—co-founders who are close friends split the stock of the company, and later one of them can't stomach the lack of income or meets her true love and moves across the country. Without the correct vesting agreements, you are destined to share the upside with someone who didn't share the risk and economic pain of your startup. There are thousands of simple mistakes ranging from bad decisions that can be fixed with money to fatal problems that can kill a financing.

Okay, so you decide to just do it right? But given that lawyers charge by the hour and do cost a lot, how can you keep this cost under control? The following are a few key ideas to keep legal costs under control and still assure the outcome is effective.

First, spend time and pick the right lawyer or law firm for your business. You want someone who has worked with hundreds of start-ups and has also worked with the companies you want to emulate as you grow and are successful. Most corporate formation mistakes aren't legal malpractice or bad lawyering; they are bad business decisions or structuring issues that may not be identified if your lawyer hasn't done the drill hundreds of times. If you are going to seek investment capital, talk to a few of your target investors for recommendations.

Next, discuss the budget with your counsel up front. Ask him how you can save on expenses by doing the non-legal legwork yourself (for example, cap tables, collecting closing signatures, preparing agreement schedules). At the same time, don't be penny-wise and pound-foolish. If no one on your team is accustomed to the level of precision required in corporate maintenance, don't take something on if you won't do it as well as the lawyers. For example, some companies manage their own option grants and records. However, if the grants or records aren't perfect, you risk having due diligence problems in a financing, or worse yet, liability to a departed employee.

Work to develop a collaborative relationship with your principal contact at the law firm. Make her a part of your mentoring team. Make sure she understands the product, the market you are chasing, your base business plan, and your team's skills. Introduce her to key members of your ecosystem and get her to talk to mentors who will be helping you make corporate or business decisions. If you do this early, most lawyers will make this investment of time on their own nickel.

Do "just in time" legal work. During the course of the first year, you will want to have legal advice on corporate formation, founders' equity, employment and consulting projects, stock options and other equity incentives, trademark and patent protection, trade secret and confidentiality issues, licensing, subscription or business model agreements, and financing strategy, including seed capital. Don't try to do everything at once. Ask your lawyer what needs to be done now, and ask how to extend your budget over time.

Don't start drafting documents before you get to resolution with your co-founders on equity splits, vesting arrangements, and basic governance concerns. If you are doing a seed financing or business transaction, do a detailed term sheet and make sure you have buy-in from all (or almost all) of the constituencies before moving to drafting the definitive legal agreements. While drafting the final documents costs money, iterating on previously drafted documents because the terms weren't clear is where companies blow legal budgets.

If you are a part of a promising startup with traction or solid proof points, or have a track record of successful entrepreneurial projects, your lawyer may be willing to take some risk on fees. If you don't fit in that category and don't have money for a retainer, consider ways to provide some upside for your lawyer's willingness to essentially be your first investor. Some firms are willing to extend payment terms for a small piece of the action. At the same time, remember that your counsel is not an investor and you probably wouldn't want him as a large equity owner in your company, so don't pick your lawyer by how much free service you can get for stock. Lawyers who are willing to take all the risk on the legal budget have free time on their hands for a reason. You will get what you pay for.

When you are designing the legal agreements to create your business model (for example, terms of service, end-user licensing arrangements, revenue-sharing arrangements, privacy policies, and so forth) don't ask for a standard form. While business lawyers have learned that drafting contracts is one exception to the age-old elementary school adage that "it doesn't pay to copy," business model agreements are one place you don't want your lawyer to say, "Sure, I will send a form right over." These business relationships are anything but standard. Spend time with a lawyer who does only technology transactions to think through your business model before having her put pen to paper. Then be willing to invest in getting it right (or close to right) the first time.

Vesting Is Good for You

Jon Fox

Jon is the founder and CTO of Intense Debate, a company that replaces your standard blog comment system with a new tool for conversation. Intense Debate raised $500,000 after completing TechStars in 2007 and was acquired by Automattic in 2008.

Many founders look at vesting as something designed purely for the investors. To them, vesting is simply a way for the investors to protect their investment and keep the founders involved in the company. While this is certainly true, vesting can also be a good thing for founders.

If you're not already familiar with vesting, the idea is that you earn your stock over some period of time as opposed to just owning it outright at the founding of the company. The length of time it takes to become fully vested can vary, but is typically four years. How frequently you vest, annually, quarterly, or monthly, also varies.

How could not receiving all your stock up front be good for a founder? Well, the big way this comes into play is with regard to co-founders. In a lot of ways, your motives are aligned with the investors in regard to your co-founders. You each want your co-founders to stick around, you want them to be motivated, and you want them to protect your own interests. Without vesting, you would be left with no recourse if one of your co-founders decided to leave the company, suddenly became unable to work, or decided he needed to take another job to earn some money. In these circumstances, the co-founder is no longer contributing to the company. If you don't have a vesting agreement, they will own all of their shares, which not only means you're working harder for less of the company, but investors will be less excited to put their money in when a large portion of the equity is tied up with someone no longer involved in the company.

We ran into a related situation at Intense Debate. We started with three founders, who all had other jobs at the time. As we gained momentum and got into TechStars, two of us decided to leave our existing jobs behind and jump 100 percent into Intense Debate. A few months later on, our third co-founder also quit his day job and focused on Intense Debate full time, but things weren't going well for him. He was forced to keep long hours without yet bringing in a paycheck since we had not yet closed our round of funding and he had no money, had moved away from his family and friends, and was straining his marriage as all these issues piled on top of one another. In the end, he decided to leave Intense Debate and move on to other things to try to get his personal life back under control.

This could have created a major problem for me and the other remaining co-founder. If the departed founder retained all of his original ownership, not only would it mean we'd have less for ourselves even though we were forced to do more of the work, but we were also afraid it would scare off potential investors. Luckily, the three of us had already agreed on a vesting schedule for ourselves. Our departing partner got only a small percentage of his original equity for the handful of months he was working with us. In the end, it all worked out. He took his shares and was very happy with the results. We retained enough ownership to make it worthwhile for ourselves, find and compensate his replacement, and close our funding. Our investors felt the value of the stock was going to the right people.

Although some founders perceive vesting as a risk, there are many cases when it can work in their favor. The key is to understand the terms of your vesting and make sure everyone is comfortable with them.

Jon's key point—that vesting protects the founders from each other—is the most important point about vesting. We often hear from entrepreneurs that their attorneys and advisors have encouraged them to own as much of their stock as they can outright so they can't get shafted by their investors. This is bad advice that shows lack of experience and perspective on the attorney's or advisor's part.

It usually takes many years for an early stage company to be successful. On Day One, all of the founders are excited about the journey they are planning. But to be successful, they have to be committed to each other and the journey. While four years is an arbitrary length of time for vesting, and we've often seen arrangements ranging from two years to eight years, it has settled out as an acceptable length of time to earn your founder's equity. Basically, if everyone is still around four years later, they've earned their share of their founder's stock.

By agreeing to vesting up front, Jon and his co-founders put the rules of engagement in place at the beginning. When one of the founders was in a position in which he couldn't continue to work with the business, the additional pressure of figuring out who owned what was eliminated since the rules were already in place. Once it was agreed that the partner would leave, there were no other decisions to make.

Jon Fox (left) and Josh Fraser came back to TechStars in 2009 to share their experiences with a new group of TechStars. And yes, Josh is all that and a bag of chips.

Now, there are cases in which founders and investor clash, and certainly plenty of cases in which founders leave the company early and lose some of their founder's stock to vesting. While this is something to be conscious of, it's usually pretty easy to find out the reputation of potential investors for how they'll approach this. If they have a reputation for dealing with situations like this fairly, you shouldn't have much to worry about. And, if they don't, you should seriously consider whether you want their investment in the first place.

Your Brother-in-Law Is Probably Not the Right Corporate Lawyer

Brad Feld

Brad is a managing director at Foundry Group and one of the co-founders of TechStars.

Photo by Scott Cejka

Entrepreneurs hate to spend money on lawyers, especially early on. I'm a good example of this—for my first company (Feld Technologies) we spent $99 to incorporate our company in Delaware, wrote our own one-page contracts, and didn't hire a lawyer until we were negotiating the sale of our company seven years later. At that point, we paid plenty because we had very little of the formal records required by the company that acquired our company. We were lucky, though, because our business was very simple, had no investors or shareholders other than the three original partners, and didn't have any litigation over the course of our business.

When I did my first angel investment (in NetGenesis) after selling my company, I got an education in how lawyers work with startup companies. I resisted it at first, but then realized that I was investing $25,000 of my hard-earned money into NetGenesis and wanted to make sure my ownership stake was properly documented. Fortunately, the company found great startup counsel (Joe Hadzima—a well-known early stage lawyer in Boston at the time). We documented everything correctly and inexpensively including vesting arrangements for the six founders which quickly turned into four with only a small amount of vested stock going to the two who bailed early.

Over three years of making angel investments, I became an expert at early stage company formation. The legal stuff made me very tired, especially with the endless, ponderous negotiations about mostly irrelevant things. In my mind, most of the negotiation and corresponding documentation could be reduced to fill in the blank exercises. However, the lawyers rarely let the business people, especially the inexperienced first-time entrepreneurs, do this.

When the lawyers are experienced at working with startups, things often take longer than they need to, but get done. However, when the lawyers aren't experienced, things can go off the rails very quickly. I've sat across the table from a variety of lawyers, including an estate lawyer, a criminal lawyer, an employment lawyer, a personal injury lawyer, and a divorce lawyer negotiating investments. While these would make for entertaining sitcoms, they were excruciating exercises in pointlessness.

All of these non-startup lawyers had some personal relationship with the entrepreneur (wife, old college friend, parent's friend, teacher), which created a deep trust relationship between the non-startup lawyer and the entrepreneur. This simply made the negotiation harder, as the phrase "You don't understand—that's not how it works" didn't mean anything to either party. Exasperation comes quickly in these situations, because there is nothing quite as bizarre as negotiating a vesting agreement with a divorce lawyer who thinks his client should "get everything, right now, no matter what."

In my experience, the best thing an entrepreneur can do in this situation is get a qualified lawyer to help him out. And the best thing the investor can do is suggest to the entrepreneur to get a qualified lawyer. This has to be done with some tact because the unqualified lawyer's first response is to tell the entrepreneur that this is a negotiating tactic. I've gotten through this a few times and in a couple of cases simply told the entrepreneur to call me if and when he was serious about doing something.

I've stopped trying to work with lawyers who aren't domain experts—it's just not worth the brain damage. A qualified lawyer can save you an enormous amount of time and trouble. One who isn't qualified, even if he's your brother-in-law, can blow up everything. Go with the qualified one every time.

To 83(b) or Not to 83(b), There Is No Question

Matt Galligan

Matt is the co-founder and CEO of SimpleGeo. He was previously the founder and CEO of Socialthing, a company that made a digital life manager that puts what you do online into one place. Socialthing raised $300,000 from several angel investors after completing TechStars in 2007, and was acquired by AOL in 2008.

There are some documents that you'll sign in the course of your life that are decidedly more important than others. Your marriage license, birth certificate of a child, and your will and testament are all perfect examples. But as a startup founder, you should add one more to your list: the Section 83(b) Election.

What is that, exactly? First, let's step back and take a refresher course in restricted stock, as all startup founders should know exactly what this is and how it affects them. Specifically, restricted stock makes use of a vesting schedule that will cause your stock to be earned by you over time, rather than all at once. While entrepreneurs don't ever start a company thinking that one of the co-founders would ever betray them, or maybe just not be quite up to snuff, it happens more often than expected. Because of that, restricted stock puts protections in place that allow the company to take back some of the stock that was granted to them in the first place if the founder doesn't workout, or decides to leave the company voluntarily. Every startup should use restricted stock with a vesting schedule to protect the founders in case one of them leaves early.

The day that your stock is granted, you don't have to report the gain as income. As soon as the stock starts to vest, however, you have to start reporting income on the increase in value on the stock you are vesting. There are a variety of things that cause an increase in the value of the stock besides normal business progress, such as when the company raises a financing at a higher valuation, or is acquired. Even if the company hasn't been acquired, any time there is an event that causes the stock to be worth more, you have to pay tax on the value of the stock. So when your company is worth $10 million on paper, and you own 10 percent of that, you'll have to pay tax on the stock accordingly. But, since the stock is valued only on paper, you don't actually have the cash to pay the tax. I know what you're probably thinking, and you're right—this sucks.

I'm here to tell you that there is another way. And, in my case, it comes from a firsthand lesson that I learned the hard way.

There is a magic document in the tax code called an 83(b) Election. This election allows for you to pay all of the tax on the stock that has been granted to you ahead of time, regardless of vesting. The reason you want to do this is because when you start your company, your stock is likely worth the least amount it will ever be worth, and the amount of tax you will need to pay is negligible.

Let's take a fake corporation, ACMESpace, as an example. When ACMESpace is founded, the stock has a value of $0.001 (a tenth of a penny). ACMESpace is successful, grows nicely over a two-year period, and is acquired by BIGCorp for $10 million. If there were a total of one million shares outstanding, each share would be worth $10.00. Obviously, that's very different from $0.001 per share. If the stock all vested upon the closing of the transaction and I owned 20 percent of the company, then I'm paying ordinary income tax (35 percent) on $2 million. Unless I took the 83(b) Election. Then I would only have to pay ordinary income tax (35 percent) on $200 and capital gains tax (15 percent but going up to 20 percent) on the rest.

We made that exact mistake when we sold my first company, Socialthing, to AOL in August 2008. When we formed the company, our lawyers gave us 83(b) Election forms to fill out, sign, and mail. But we never sent them to the IRS. And here's the kicker: you must file the election within 30 days of your stock grant or lose the option forever. So the scenario described here became all too real. Because we neglected to send in a very simple document, we ended up paying a lot more tax than we needed to when we sold our company.

The moral of the story is this: if you have already started your company, double check with your legal counsel that you have filed your 83(b) Election. If you have started, or are getting ready to start your company: make sure that just after you prepare your restricted stock grants, you get your 83(b) Election signed and filed. Don't make the same mistake we made.

While Matt is good-natured today about the mistake he and his founders made, it was painful at the time we all encountered it. AOL and Socialthing had agreed on the terms of an acquisition and the lawyers were drafting documents and putting together the Socialthing diligence material. Brad was at his house in Homer, Alaska, and remembers the call with Matt well since he was at a gas station filling up his car when the call came in. Matt said, "Brad, what's an 83(b) Election?" Brad replied, "Matt, please don't tell me you don't have an 83(b) Election." Matt answered, "I don't have an 83(b) Election. What is it?"

Over the next few days, in addition to the normal stress generated by a transaction, Matt had to endure a number of calls with Brad and lawyers sorting through the stock vesting dynamics, the price of the stock at various points in time, and ultimately a spreadsheet that showed the tax implications of not having the 83(b) Election. While Matt and his co-founders were frustrated that they didn't have the election, they also acknowledged that the lawyers had given them the docs and the envelopes to mail them in—they just didn't ever get around to it.

In the end, it all worked out fine. Matt and his co-founders paid more tax than they would have if they had made the 83(b) Election, but the deal closed and everyone was still very happy.

Today, when someone in TechStars asks us about 83(b) Elections, we just say "Go talk to Matt Galligan." That usually takes care of it.

Matt Galligan and the rest of Socialthing discuss their acquisition by AOL during Demo Day in Summer 2008.

THEME 7: WORK–LIFE BALANCE

Most of us who play this game called entrepreneurship have an amazing work ethic. It's really hard to succeed as a startup founder if you don't. But in our experience, the best entrepreneurs also know how to disconnect and unwind. They find a balance that works for them and it makes them stronger entrepreneurs.

We often work with young first-time founders at TechStars. Most of them have bought into the myth that you have to work *constantly* in order to succeed. We think you just have to work *productively*, and there's a huge difference.

To work productively, you need to occasionally recharge your batteries. Some people can do this by just taking a week off once in a while. Others can do it by going on a bike ride. Work and life balance takes many forms because each of us needs to find our own way of achieving it.

Even in the hectic 90-day period that constitutes TechStars, we try to provide balance. We organize a few hikes, a bar crawl here or there, perhaps even a night outdoors for a movie at the Red Rocks Amphitheater. On the day before investor day we ask the founders to take the day off and relax. We've even been known to surprise the founders by bringing in massage therapists close to investor day. Everything happens fast at TechStars, but these little things actually add to the productivity.

The bottom line is that without balance, you're sure to fall down sooner or later.

Discover Work–Life Balance

Brad Feld

Brad is a managing director at Foundry Group and one of the co-founders of TechStars.

T he challenge of work–life balance is a central theme for many people, especially entrepreneurs. It took me 15 years, a failed first marriage, and my current wife almost calling it quits for me to realize that I had to figure out what work–life balance meant to me. Today, I can comfortably say that I have a major clue and my life is dramatically better for it.

I started my first company when I was 19 and in college at MIT. I was obsessive, worked incredibly hard, and, while I generally had a lot of fun, was almost always maxed out. This manifested itself in many ways, including always being overcommitted, regularly being exhausted, having a failed marriage when I was 24, and physically changing, according to one of my best friends, from "skinny Brad" to FOB ("fat older Brad.")

I was very successful at the work I did during this time. The first company I created, Feld Technologies, was acquired by a public company. I helped start or finance a number of other companies that went on to be acquired or go public. I co-founded a venture capital firm. I was well known and respected within the entrepreneurial community both for what I had accomplished and what I was working on.

However, I had absolutely no balance in my life. I was on the road from Monday to Friday, arriving home exhausted at the end of the day Friday. My wife, Amy, got "the dregs" over the weekend. I'd sleep a lot, spend time in front of my computer getting caught up on all the crap I didn't get to during the week, and when we went out, I'd always be tired and withdrawn. The burnout cycle continued; every six months I'd completely crash from the effort. On one vacation to Hawaii with friends I slept 20 hours a day for the first four days—so much that Amy thought something was physically wrong with me. I drank too much, I struggled with my weight, and I felt physically crappy. I loved my work, but I couldn't see past it.

At age 34 when, on a long weekend with friends when I was completely absent and struggling to get through a difficult deal (for a company that eventually failed), Amy turned to me and said "I'm done. I'm not mad; I just don't want to do this anymore. You either have to change, or it's over."

That woke me up! We spent the rest of the weekend talking about what change meant. I knew that this wasn't a warning. After that weekend, we created a set of well-defined rules that have evolved over time. As I discovered what balance meant to me, the rules evolved into a set of habits that include spend time away, life dinner, segment space, be present, and meditate. The following are examples of each.

> *Spend Time Away:* Amy and I take a week-long vacation each quarter (which we fondly refer to as "Qx Vacation" depending on which quarter of the year it is) where we completely disappear. No cell phone, no e-mail, no computer, no conference calls. My assistant knows how to find me in case of an emergency; otherwise, I'm completely unavailable for the week.

> *Life Dinner:* We have a standing date on the first day of every month that we call life dinner. We'll occasionally invite friends; we often have dinner alone. We have a ritual in which we give each other a gift ranging in value from nominal or silly (a fart machine) to expensive or romantic (jewelry). We

spend the evening talking about the previous month and about the month to come, grounding ourselves in our current reality.

Segment Space: We have several homes, including one in the mountains of Boulder, Colorado, and one in the small town of Homer, Alaska. Both have nice office areas that are clearly separated from the rest of the house. We only have telephones in the offices and, by some delightful fluke of nature, our cell phones don't work in our Boulder house. We treat our houses as a retreat from the world and, while we do plenty of working at home, where we do this is separate and distinct from the rest of the house.

Be Present: One of Amy's lines to me is "Brad, be a person." This is a signal to me that I'm not present in the moment, that something is troubling me, or simply that I'm tired. Whenever I'm not present, it only takes a short phrase to pull me back from wherever I've drifted off to.

Meditate: I use the word meditate metaphorically—everyone should meditate their own way. At age 35, I became a marathoner—the 6 to 10 hours a week I run is my current form of meditation. I'm also a voracious reader and the 10 hours a week I read extends my meditation time. Do whatever you want, but spend some of your time on yourself.

The habits have created a structure for my life that not only encourages but reinforces a healthy work–life balance. My work, which used to overwhelm everything else I did, is still a central part of my life. It is no longer my singular focus, however, nor is it the most important thing to me anymore. The balance that I've discovered has helped me understand the value of other things, which has made my work and, more importantly, my life, much more rewarding.

Practice Your Passion

Eran Egozy

Eran is the co-founder and CTO of Harmonix Music Systems, the creators of the video games Guitar Hero and Rock Band. He has been a TechStars mentor since 2009.

Photo Courtesy of Harmonix/MTV

I have two passions: music and building things. When I look back at what has happened in my life, it all comes back to those two things. At age six, my parents got me Legos. At 11, I started playing the clarinet. At 15, I wrote a machine language program for my Apple IIe to play back digital music with six-note polyphony. I painstakingly entered each note from a score of Beethoven's Ninth Symphony in machine code. While this was the first time I combined my two passions, I didn't realize I was doing it, although in retrospect it all makes sense.

After undergraduate and graduate school at MIT, where I got degrees in Engineering and Music, I started Harmonix with my friend Alex Rigopulos. Unlike some entrepreneurs, we didn't start the company to be entrepreneurs. We started the company because we had a mission: to let anyone in the world experience the joy of making music. Starting a company happened to be the only way we knew to fulfill that mission. Alex was the business guy. I was the tech guy. I got to build software that makes music again just like when I was 15.

Passion is often an overused word that loses its meaning, especially when attached to marketing statements such as "Your potential. Our passion." To find your passion is to find those few things in your life that provide emotional satisfaction in and of themselves. Instead of hating your job, like many people do, imagine being able to work on your passion as your job. Now imagine being able to start a company doing the same thing.

Harmonix had two distinct time periods: 1995 to 2005 (before Guitar Hero), and 2005 to the present. Those first 10 years were long and difficult. We raised about $10 million during that time and had very little revenue. By 2004, we had barely gotten to be a break-even business. I am often asked how I kept going when our prospect for success was so bleak. The answer is simple—I fundamentally loved what I was doing! The doing part gave us enough satisfaction that success in business was not necessary to keep us motivated.

When Guitar Hero became a hit, we were called an overnight success. It was a really long night—10 years in the making. But our passion for doing what we loved every day made it a great 10 years.

Harmonix is one of those great "overnight" success stories that give us chills every time we think about it. Eran was a fraternity brother of Brad's but they didn't know each other, since they were almost 10 years apart in age. When Eran was thinking about starting Harmonix, he recalled that Brad had started a company and reached out to him. Brad was immediately supportive of Eran and Alex and helped put together the first angel financing for the company. The investors in this round were a Who's Who of Brad's friends—his first business partner, his father, a friend of his father's, the two guys who bought Brad's first company, and a couple of successful angel investors who were investing alongside Brad. Basically, your perfect angel syndicate—a bunch of entrepreneurs and friends who wanted to support two young entrepreneurs with an amazing vision.

A decade passed. Brad would periodically get together with Eran and Alex when he was in Boston. Every now and then something came up when they sought out his advice. But most of the angels that invested alongside Brad lost track of the company. Ten years is a long time.

Suddenly, Guitar Hero became a massive success. It was fun to play the game and talk about being an investor, but it was hard to tell what it meant. One day, MTV acquired Harmonix. When the deal was announced, the angels were stunned, because it was a bigger success than any of them had imagined. Several had actually forgotten they even owned stock in the company and were blown away by the check they got.

All of this was a result of the efforts of Eran, Alex, and the Harmonix team they put together. As determined entrepreneurs, they probably would have figured out how to get funding if Brad and his gang hadn't shown up. But they did, and it made it even sweeter for everyone, especially when the angels realized that Eran and Alex were just practicing their passion all along.

Follow Your Heart

Mark Solon

Mark is a managing partner at Highway 12 Ventures in Boise, Idaho. He's been a TechStars mentor since 2007. Highway 12 is an investor in several TechStars companies, including Everlater and SendGrid.

Photo Courtesy of Highway 12 Ventures

I met my wife Pam in a coffee shop in Boston's South End in 1993. Having lived in big cities my whole life (New York, Chicago, San Francisco, and Boston), I was smitten with this gal, who grew up in the small town of Boise, Idaho, and had a zest for life like few I've ever met. I asked her to marry me as soon as I had saved enough for a ring. Over the next seven years, we moved from our tiny apartment in the South End to Bunker Hill and then up to Marblehead, where we bought a creaky 150-year-old Victorian near the ocean that needed a ton of work. She was working at a cool startup in the city and I became a partner at a boutique private equity firm. We had a daughter in late 1998 and had another child on the way in early 2000.

Life seemed like a fairy tale. There was only one problem. I'd lie awake at night and dream about living in Idaho. From the time we met, we spent most of our vacation time back in Boise and I quickly fell in love with Idaho. Having lived with concrete under my feet for my first 35 years, I felt like I was in heaven every time we were there and each time I got on a plane back to Boston, I'd think to myself, "If only I could figure out a way to live there." I never shared those thoughts with Pam. While we had talked about moving to the Pacific Northwest someday (she had worked in Seattle for five years after college and loved it), we never really had a serious talk about living in Idaho. Yet more and more, I'd lie awake at night thinking about getting the nerve to ditch life in the big city and all of its trappings for a simpler life in the mountains of Idaho. Yet there we were, parents of a one-year-old and eight months pregnant with our second child. I knew that if I didn't pull the trigger soon, it would never happen.

On Sunday, April 11, 2000, I woke Pam on her birthday and said, "Happy birthday, let's move to Boise." She looked at me like I had lost my mind. "What in the world are you going to do in Boise?" she asked. "I have no idea, let's just move there and we'll figure it out." We talked about it all day. We called her mother in Boise and talked to her about it too and by that evening we committed to the idea. Twenty-four hours later, I walked into my office and said I was moving to Idaho. My partner, Leon (who is Russian), asked me where in Massachusetts the town of Idaho was. We put our house on the market that week and I flew out to Boise to start some business networking while Pam started winding down our life in Boston. Networking in Boise was pretty easy. Pam is a fourth-generation Idahoan and with Boise being a small town, her mom knew many of the business leaders, who proved to be incredibly accessible. I had no idea what I was going to do career-wise, but as I met with more and more folks from the business community, a pattern emerged: "With your background, why don't you start a venture fund?"

I hadn't really thought of that. I mean, venture funds only existed in places like Boston and Silicon Valley, right? It was then that fate, or what Pam calls "trusting the universe" started to kick in. Over the next couple of weeks I met two people who would help solidify my notion to actually start Idaho's first institutionally backed venture capital fund. First, I met Jim Hawkins. Jim is a well-respected and incredibly connected native Idahoan who was about to retire as the director of commerce of Idaho and he was also a successful lifelong entrepreneur. After a long meeting, he said to me, "With your background and my contacts, let's start a venture fund." It was then that

I started to seriously consider this as a career option. Next, I was introduced by a friend to Matt Harris, who was in the process of starting Village Ventures, a unique venture fund designed to support smaller funds in regional markets. By providing back-office support and a strong network of funds to share best practices, Village Ventures was a natural fit with which to partner. The rest, as they say, is history. Over the next year, Jim and I were able to raise a $25 million fund focused on investing in the most promising high-growth companies in the Intermountain West. Phil Reed joined us early on and we had some modest success in our first fund which allowed us to raise a subsequent $75 million fund in late 2006.

Even though some consider Highway 12 Ventures a success, to me it still feels like a startup. I relate more to the entrepreneurs of TechStars than I do to my peers at the big venture capital firms. For me, I consider our first fund to be our seed money and second fund our Series A round. I consider myself as much an entrepreneur as anyone that we've backed. There's still a lot of wood to chop for Highway 12 Ventures.

When I spend time in the TechStars bunker during the summer, I'm completely energized and inspired by the small teams that have dropped everything and moved to Boulder to pursue their dreams. I look at someone like Mark O'Sullivan, who left his family in Canada and see a little bit of myself. Or Kevin Mann from Graphic.ly, who has been fighting immigration issues and left his family and friends in the United Kingdom to take advantage of being chosen for TechStars. But the guys I admire most are Nate and Natty from Everlater. Despite having terrific post-collegiate lucrative jobs on Wall Street that could have served as launching pads for even more lucrative careers, these two childhood friends chucked it all and set out on a year-long around-the-world adventure because the universe was calling to them.

As I got to know them last summer, I was very drawn to these two young men. They didn't view leaving the comfort of high-paying jobs as a risk; for them, the risk was not following their hearts. They were young and single without any obligations. They'd saved some money and knew they had an opportunity of a lifetime to see the world before the tangled web of jobs, wives, children, and more serious responsibilities would make that much more difficult. They believed in themselves and knew they would land on their feet when they returned.

Here's where the real magic happens. Frustrated with the lack of tools to adequately share their wonderful travel experience with friends and family, they hatched a plan to start Everlater upon their return. When they finished their around-the-world adventure, they moved in with their parents, taught themselves to code, and launched an incredibly cool web site to help travelers better share their experiences with their friends and family. It's a fantastic product and they're well on their way to building a terrific business together.

The moral of the story is easy: When you follow your heart, good things usually happen. We have a very short stay on this spinning orb and I believe life is way too short to be stuck in a career that doesn't fulfill you. There's really nothing to risk by starting your own company because we all know fundamentally that you can't take it with you. I believe with all my heart that you have to trust that the wind knows where it's going. I guess that's why I'm such a fan of TechStars; because I believe that all of the founders subscribe to that very same notion.

Mark's story of following his heart to Boise, Idaho, appeals to us because it's very similar to how each of us ended up in Boulder, Colorado.

Brad and his wife, Amy, were trapped in Boston. Amy grew up in Alaska and Brad grew up in Dallas, so Boston wasn't home to either of them. On cold, gloomy days in Boston they'd talk about moving somewhere else to live, but the inertia of having gone to school in Boston and subsequently building a life and a business there kept them from taking action. But they kept talking and whenever they traveled around the United States, which was often, they kept their eyes open for a place to live. They passed through Boulder on a December day in 1993 when it was 60 degrees and sunny and both said to the other, "Remember this." After Brad sold his first company, he committed to Amy to leave Boston by the time he was 30; two months before his birthday Amy informed him that she was moving to Boulder and he could join her if he wanted to.

David moved to Boulder because of a pizza dinner. He and his two co-founders were having dinner at Pizzeria Uno in Tempe, Arizona, when they started jotting down cities on a napkin. Each of them were living in a separate city at the time, but they knew they wanted to be together to help them get serious about their startup. Because they intended to sell public safety software nationally, the group decided that they would pick a location that would allow them to get to both coasts with some regularity. But they also wanted to live somewhere that they would personally enjoy. Boulder was the only remaining city on the list after all vetoes were exercised.

Turn Work into Play

Howard Lindzon

Howard is the founder and CEO of Stock-Twits. He was previously the creator of Wallstrip (acquired by CBS). He runs a fund called Social Leverage and has been a TechStars mentor since 2007.

I am passionate about the financial markets, so many of my start-ups have been fun. In 2006, I started Wallstrip, which was a daily three-minute web videoblog covering one great stock at a time. I invest in trends, and our goal with Wallstrip was to unlock the best stocks that were trending up and think about why. I wanted Wallstrip to do for the stock market what Jon Stewart had done for politics and news.

I believe magical things can happen when you can invest where your passion lies. Entrepreneurs need an edge. No matter what the startup, the work is endless and will be tedious at times. It helps to know your industry inside out. If you choose an area to work in which you have passion and deep knowledge, you will know more about the opportunities that lie ahead and the products that could lead to profits. The roadblocks you hit will seem solvable. Your daily progress will be easily measurable and you will know when you are on the right track.

I knew exactly the product that I needed to deliver for Wallstrip to gain attention and an audience. We built it and delivered it every day, we worked like crazy together as a team to do an amazing job, and we created one of the first popular videoblogs. As we gained momentum and visibility, a buyer for the company emerged. When we started Wallstrip, we didn't build it to sell it, but my best trades have always come from a good investment premise. That is just how it worked.

I always knew that Wallstrip was not enough for me. While it was a good start on changing the way people look at and discuss markets, my work on this problem was not done. In 2008 I co-founded Stocktwits, leveraging the microblogging platform Twitter to build a lasting community for people who loved stocks and markets. Stocktwits is amazingly fun but it is also incredibly hard work. In fact, I've never worked harder in my life. But I'm having a blast.

Today Stocktwits has a dozen employees, a huge community on top of Twitter, our own microblogging platform, revenue, and an early lead in the way new stock and market discussions take place. The team is having a ton of fun while working incredibly hard to build an important company. And yes, we're hard at play.

The greatest entrepreneurs often talk about how much they love what they do. It's similar to some great athletes who are absolutely joyful when they are at the peak of their game. There's often a grind that comes with creating any company or practicing over and over again to master a sport. But there's a magic moment when it all comes together. At that moment, the work is play. And that's when amazing things often happen.

Source: Photo Courtesy of Bill Erickson

Howard Lindzon leads a discussion with the TechStars founders in 2008.

Get Out from behind Your Computer

Seth Levine

Seth is a managing director at Foundry Group and has been a TechStars mentor since 2007.

One generally pictures the world of business primarily taking place in offices—people working diligently behind their desks either on their computers or on the phone and taking meetings in conference rooms. Heading out of the office has typically meant traveling to someone else's office for a meeting or heading to lunch to talk shop. In recent years, I've been experimenting with expanding this notion of out-of-office meetings to include some places that, while not typically thought of as business settings, have proven to be both very productive and, as a side benefit, extremely enjoyable.

For me, this has primarily taken the form of bike rides in and around the foothills of Boulder, Colorado, where I live. While I typically do this with others, I've also found that over the course of a lunch ride alone I've gained clarity on business issues that had often been percolating with little result for days or weeks. In the case of heading out with colleagues, the casual nature of a hike or ride is the perfect environment to catch up on business.

My efforts at lunch rides and meetings started with Ari Newman, the co-founder and CEO of TechStars 2007 participant Filtrbox. The idea was purely social. Ari is an accomplished rider and we thought it would be fun to head out together for a ride. I quickly realized that to keep up with him on our rides, however, I needed to get him talking. So I started to ask him questions about his business, which was something I knew Ari, like all entrepreneurs, was happy to talk at length about. This was a natural extension of the more formal time we were spending together through the TechStars program, as I served as lead mentor to Filtrbox during their TechStars summer and continued working with the company after they exited the program and received institutional funding. Not only did these discussions have the desired effect of slowing Ari down, but our rides proved to be perfect settings to talk about the progress of the company. Away from the office, riding the hills of Boulder, it was easier for us to collectively gain perspective on the business that we weren't able to when we were physically confined by the walls of the Filtrbox office.

While my 2008 TechStars company was not as athletic and our meetings took place in the more typical format in a conference room, Ari and I continued to work on Filtrbox that summer on our regular rides. As I started mentoring Everlater in TechStars program of 2009, cycling had become a meaningful part of my summer agenda. With a large group of cyclists involved in the Boulder tech scene, there were regular lunchtime rides throughout the summer (the group, called Geeks on Wheels, used Twitter to arrange rides.) With this as the backdrop, it was natural to make cycling a central part of my work with Everlater's founders, Nate Abbott and Natty Zola. Nate, Natty, and I scheduled regular weekly rides (sometimes several times a week) and while we didn't keep a formal agenda, each ride had a number of topics planned out for us to cover. In this way, we worked through many of the early challenges the business faced as it moved from idea to reality in the course of the summer of 2009. Our typical rides lasted from 60 to 90 minutes during which time we were able to focus on the business without interruption. And while getting some fresh air helps bring perspective, it's hard to avoid thinking about problems in a new way when you're out of the office, surrounded by the beauty of the Boulder foothills while your mind is completely clear.

While one obvious side benefit of these activities was getting in shape, I also found that cycling with Ari, Nate, Natty, and others was a great way to get to know them personally. These friendships, which started in TechStars, but which were nurtured over hours in the saddle, have been some of my greatest joys from participating in the TechStars program.

These days, when confronted by a particularly challenging issue, it's not uncommon for me to grab my running or cycling shoes and head out for a hike or ride. The clarity and perspective that a little time outside the office can provide is priceless.

We periodically hear our entrepreneur friends from the East or West Coast make comments like "No one in Boulder really works very hard—everyone just wants to live there so they can mountain bike and ski." The enlightened among us no longer get defensive when we hear things like this; rather, we just smirk and avoid engaging in what is inevitably a silly conversation.

The beauty of living in a place like Boulder is that you are minutes away from whatever you want. Your commute is short—fifteen minutes at most unless you bike or run to work, in which case you don't really care how long it is since you are biking or running. Some of the greatest hiking trails in the world are within a five-minute walk of downtown Boulder. And if you want to go skiing at some of the best resorts in the world, it's less than 90 minutes away.

As Seth's essay shows, getting out from behind your computer and working to solve hard issues are not mutually exclusive. One of Brad's mentors, Len Fassler, would start every hard conversation with "Let's go for a walk." Brad and Len covered many miles over the years they worked together walking, talking, enjoying being out in the world, and figuring out answers to whatever they were struggling with.

Seth, Ari, Nate, and Natty show us another way to mix work and play. And their results as entrepreneurs demonstrate how successful you can be when doing this.

Stay Healthy

Andy Smith

Andy is the co-founder and CEO of Daily-Burn, the premier fitness social network for detailed tracking, online accountability, and motivation, which raised $500,000 from angel investors after completing Tech-Stars in 2008. DailyBurn was acquired by IAC in 2010.

Photo Courtesy of TwoWeekIn.com

In an environment like TechStars, a lot of work has to be done in a short period of time. For three months, you work around 18 hours a day, seven days a week. This way of life is not sustainable, but for a short-term burst, it is almost always necessary. Starting a new company is a full-out sprint, but building a lasting company is a marathon, and you need to train for both.

Just like preparing for any race or athletic event, you need to prepare your body for the extra stress that happens when you start a business. Proper nutrition, exercise, and rest are more important during periods of high stress. The following are some specific tips to minimize your stress levels and maximize your output during the early stages of a startup.

First, exercise five to six days a week. Even 20 minutes a day of high intensity exercise, such as a mix of cardio and weight training, will decrease your stress and increase your focus. While I recommend fast, high intensity workouts such as Crossfit, the most important thing is that you do something!

Next, eat right most of the time. You should aim to eat healthy meals at least 80 percent of the time. The best things to eat are lean meat, vegetables, nuts and seeds, and some fruit. When you go grocery shopping, stick to the outside perimeter of the store for fresh (not processed) food choices and don't eat anything that has more than 10 ingredients listed on the label. If one or more of the ingredients has a word you cannot spell or you don't recognize as food, don't eat it.

Don't forget to sleep. You should aim for at least seven hours of sleep a night. Don't binge on caffeine. An all-nighter once in a while is okay if you are young, but don't do it every other day.

Finally, at least once a week, step back and think about the big picture. As an entrepreneur, it is very easy to get lost in the day-to-day madness of starting your company and lose sight of the bigger picture of your life. This applies to fitness, too; you don't just wake up fat and unhealthy one day—you get there by not making the day-to-day choices that are best for you. A healthy you will ultimately be better for your company.

Now that we are in our 40s (Brad is 44 and David is 42), we appreciate this advice even more. When we were in our 20s, we were both indestructible. All-nighter—no big deal. Four hours of sleep night after night? Whatever. Red-eyes—bring them on. A gigantic plate of fried fish, clams, and oysters followed by three scoops of ice cream. Yum.

All that extra weight came from somewhere. We are tired more often. It's satisfying to get eight hours of sleep on a regular basis. Six beers sounds like five too many.

Take care of yourself. Nothing lasts forever.

Several of the TechStars from 2008 take a break for a quick hike.

Get Away from It All

Amy Batchelor

Amy is a writer and philanthropist. She is married to Brad Feld (for better or for worse).

If you're like most startup entrepreneurs, you work every day—Sundays, holidays, your birthday. This seems necessary since so much depends on you; but it's not. It's actually a terrible way to live, and simply isn't sustainable over the arc of an entrepreneurial lifetime. When you always have your head down and are focused only on what's right in front of you, it's impossible to develop perspective and ensure that you're heading toward the right goal on the horizon. Being as goal-driven and structured with your vacation time as you are with your work is an important step toward achieving that elusive work–life balance—and make no mistake, achieving balance is a huge achievement.

When you're caught up in the adrenaline rush, you get a lot done, but you also raise your cortisol levels and other stress hormones. Along with the likely sleep deprivation you're experiencing, this is bad for you. Taking a break, especially from all of your electronic devices, allows your brain and body to recover so that you can plunge back into the fray. Play is good for you physically, emotionally, and mentally.

My husband and I went to a hiking boot camp in which they had you do a life balance self-assessment by dividing your days into a pie chart of hours of work, play, and sleep. This can be a very revealing exercise. In a startup entrepreneurial mode, it's unlikely and probably not even desirable that every day divides nicely into three slices of eight hours of work, play, and sleep. It's worth trying, however, to have a graph that over the course of a year includes big peak work times and then some high curves for rest and relaxation, restoration and rejuvenation, and recalibration. Even if you define your work as play, which is often a fortuitous consequence of being an entrepreneur, it's still wise to change gears on a regular basis. My husband and I have different definitions of his work. He often does define it as play; but I define his work as any time he's not available to play with me.

Years ago, when he had nearly exhausted my tanks of patience and support, we negotiated a contract in which we would get away from it all for an entire week every quarter: no work, no phone calls, no e-mail, no electronic devices—no exceptions. A week every three months seems like a lot of time, especially in our American culture in which many people don't take even the two weeks they're allowed. But if you're working 70-hour work weeks 48 weeks a year instead of 52 weeks a year, you're only missing 280 hours out of a possible 3,640 hours, or about an 8 percent commitment to time for yourself. When you look at it like that, four weeks a year doesn't seem like very much after all. When we first started trying this, the first few days of withdrawal from the constant stimulation of electronic input weren't pretty to watch. Now it's easier. We've developed a good habit of going away over the past 10 years or so, and since we have a history of choosing to disconnect, it's easier to make rare exceptions to the no-work rules.

There are excellent pragmatic reasons to go away. Getting ready to go always entails a mad burst of rushing around and desk clearing and last-minute fits of excessive efficiency. I always clear my desk before I go away so that I won't dread returning, or at least won't dread seeing my desk even if I'm loathe to leave the beach. It's astonishing how much you can get done when an airplane departure is your deadline.

Returning with a clear, well-rested mind results in very high levels of productivity, and you'll have renewed enthusiasm for your work. As an entrepreneur, some of the most valuable work you do in your company is to create a healthy culture. Work smarter, not harder. Work hard, work healthy. You can be a role model to all of the other energetic hard-working people in your company, and show that although everyone's contributions are important, no one is indispensable, not even you. It's important to have teams with whom you can trust that things will work in your absence. Building a company with systems in place in case there is a genuine emergency while you're away is a good growth model. You'll be amazed how rarely a real emergency arises that requires you to leave your pina colada and Dan Brown paperback by the pool to take a phone call. It's a good ego adjustment to realize that your company can continue without you.

The emotional, spiritual, foofy reasons to go away are at least as important as considerations of increased efficiency. If you're in a committed relationship, sharing an experience of sleeping as much as you want with no alarm clock, and then spending entire days without any calendar appointments is a delightful chance to remember that you enjoy being together, doing things together, and doing nothing together. It also restores the patience and support levels of your partner, and demonstrates that your relationship really is important to you, even in the midst of creating an entrepreneurial venture. If you're not in a committed relationship, go away and take some friends. Social networks that involve eye contact and no typing and lots of laughter are just as important in the twenty-first century as in the last one.

THE EVOLUTION OF TECHSTARS

We've been very fortunate that TechStars has wildly exceeded our expectations. People around the world have noticed, and many have become incredibly interested in TechStars. Many of them have reached out to us for assistance. We have actively tried to help them understand and replicate our mentorship-driven and community-oriented model.

Since the beginning, TechStars has taken an open source approach. We have publicly shared our model seed funding documents, our results, and our philosophies about startups, many of which you have just read.

What began as a simple experiment has now grown into a meaningful part of the startup ecosystem in the three communities that TechStars now calls home. What follows are a few of the stories of how TechStars started, why it has expanded, and what might come next.

What Motivated Me to Start TechStars?

David Cohen

David is a co-founder and the CEO of TechStars.

I'm often asked what my motivations were for starting TechStars. While I think that TechStars represents a better way of angel investing, there are other big reasons that TechStars was born in 2006. We wanted to see more interesting startups happening in Boulder over time. We thought that TechStars could bring both new talent and national attention to Boulder, and it has. We thought it would be a great way to engage the best and brightest from all over the country to come to Boulder and experience why so many of us fall in love with it. We thought it would fill a pipeline of lifelong entrepreneurs that we could nurture and invest in over time. And finally, selfishly, I simply couldn't think of anything that would be more fun than working on 10 interesting new startups every summer.

TechStars is mentorship-driven. We bring together the most accomplished serial entrepreneurs and investors from Colorado, Silicon Valley, Boston, New York, and elsewhere. Together, we focus on 10 companies that are selected from more than 600 that apply for each session. These mentors give freely of their time during the summer, helping the companies refine their business models, introducing them to early customers and partners, and helping them raise capital from investors.

Why do the mentors get so involved and do what they do? Why does the whole town rally around the startups that go through the program, helping them shape their products and promoting them broadly? Why does everyone in Colorado seem to ask, "How can I help?" It's because in a larger sense, TechStars is really all about community. In Boulder entrepreneurship circles, there is a genuine desire to see others succeed and a general belief that karma matters. There's a sense that together we're building something here, and that we're all a meaningful part of it.

And it's coming back around. From the 2007 class of 10 companies, five have already been acquired. One of those companies was Socialthing, which sold to AOL in 2008. Since then, AOL has opened an office here in Boulder, employing more people. Socialthing founder Matt Galligan has now persuaded Joe Stump (former lead architect at Digg) to move to Boulder and join him in his second business, SimpleGeo. When Matt and his co-founders sold Socialthing, they didn't forget about the community that helped them to be so successful. They donated 1 percent of their equity to the Entrepreneurs Foundation of Colorado and together with Intense Debate and Filtrbox helped generate more than $100,000 for local nonprofit organizations.

One of the things that I'm most proud of is the increase in mentorship throughout the entire entrepreneurial community in Boulder. We've created a culture of sustained mentorship, and because of this Boulder is going to be a real force for some time to come. We hope that we can have a similar impact on the other communities that we now call home.

TechStars has wildly exceeded my own expectations in so many dimensions. Simply put, it reminds me of every successful startup I've ever been a part of.

David Cohen takes notes on Matt Mullenweg's thoughts about each company after a day of meetings during the summer of 2008.

Why TechStars Started in Boulder

Jason Mendelson

Jason is a managing director at Foundry Group and has been a TechStars mentor since 2007.

While Silicon Valley may get most of the press for having a strong startup ecosystem, Boulder is a great place to start a new business. In fact, Boulder has many qualities that really set it apart from other geographies. So what makes it so great?

First, Boulder is incredibly supportive. There is a huge sense of community. While there is a ton of activity, there might not be a place that is as supportive as Boulder is. Instead of competition, there is collaboration. Whether it's the Boulder New Tech Meetup, the Boulder OpenCoffee Club, Boulder Software Club, or Silicon Flatirons events, the entire community, including entrepreneurs, investors, students, service professionals, professors, and others involved in the startup ecosystem share their knowledge and experience to help others. This sense of giving back is a key characteristic of Boulder, and there is no better example of this than the success of TechStars.

Next, Boulder's culture encourages a healthy work–life balance. Boulder has an incredible amount to offer with easy access to mountains, hiking trails, and natural beauty. People actually have time to focus and concentrate on things outside of work. It's definitely got a slightly saner pace than in Silicon Valley. It's not that people don't work hard—they do—but there is a certain amount of balance that isn't completely explainable unless you live here. For residents,

Jason Mendelson giving the skeptical look known around TechStars as "The Jason Mendelson."

it means that the hours they do work are more efficient and their brains feel sharper.

Boulder is centrally located. Startups are increasingly national and international organizations. For anyone who has flown from San Francisco to New York, they know it's not a fun trip. One can take a day trip from Boulder to New York, an impossible feat from the Bay Area, at least without a private jet. While an East Coast day trip is not the most fun one can have, the couple of hours that one saves means that meetings the day of arrival aren't nearly as brutal. And getting back and forth to the Bay Area is a relatively painless experience.

Finally, Boulder is an entrepreneurially vibrant community. There are loads of startups in Boulder. The entire Front Range of Colorado has had many successful companies created; many of these entrepreneurs are now working on their next big thing. The community applauds these efforts and supports the necessary risk taking for creating new ventures. With engaged universities that have integrated themselves into the fabric of the ecosystem along with the required service providers and angel and professional investors, there is a well-developed economy to help great entrepreneurs create great companies.

So while Silicon Valley may get more press, there are other great places to start companies, such as Boulder. Come visit—I bet you won't want to leave.

How TechStars Came to Boston

Bill Warner

Bill is the founder of Avid Technology (the pioneer in video editing software) and Wildfire Communications. He is also a co-founder of TechStars in Boston.

first heard about TechStars when I was introduced to David Cohen in 2008. I was looking at investing in EventVue, a TechStars company, and I was curious to find out who and what was behind the program.

Since 2004, I have worked with five startups as an angel investor. My focus with these five companies was to help the entrepreneurs align their invention with their own intention. My thought was that if you get the very early stage right, then the rest will follow. I worked hard with each company founder and helped them align their product designs with the needs they were serving and with the energy that drove them to invent in the first place. I was excited to see how it all worked, but in the end, the results were disappointing. Of the five companies I invested in, one got venture capital and then ran smack into the downturn. It was ultimately sold at a low price although its product is still being sold by the acquiring company. While I felt that overall I made huge progress with the various entrepreneurs on aligning founder intention with the actual invention, alas, that wasn't enough and I had to report a zero for five track record on creating sustainable companies.

While any textbook on entrepreneurship will tell you that team is crucial, I had to find this out for myself. I learned that one founder has a hard time sustaining the energy needed to make a startup happen. And I found that one main advisor is also not enough.

When I started talking to David Cohen, and later with Brad Feld, I felt like TechStars answered so many of the deficiencies I had experienced in my much-too-lonely journey with these entrepreneurs. The TechStars model brings a group of companies together (around 10 each year) in a compressed time to get a product to market. It focused on teams of two, three, and sometimes more founders. TechStars works by focusing an amazing amount of mentor talent on each company, with an approach that makes it easy for mentors to select which teams interest them, and vice versa. Finally, the focus on mentorship has an energizing effect on the mentor community; getting them involved, more engaged, and excited about what is going on in their backyard. This spurs the local entrepreneurial economy.

After our first meeting at the end of 2008, we all believed that Boston would be a perfect venue for an expansion of TechStars beyond Boulder. But a lot of different things needed to align in order to make TechStars Boston happen in time for a June 2009 start. The most crucial of these steps was finding Shawn Broderick to be the managing director. He then took the ball and worked out the rest, with help from David and Brad. In a remarkably short time, Shawn and the team found a location, finalized investors and mentors, and chose the nine companies for TechStars Boston 2009.

At the end of the program, the companies presented their products and plans in front of a packed room with over 300 people at Microsoft's New England Research and Development (NERD) center. As I listened to each presentation, I saw the alignment between the entrepreneur's energy and their products that I had been seeking in my solo work. I saw teams of entrepreneurs supporting each other. I saw hundreds of people and investors in the audience ready to support these new efforts. And I felt really satisfied that all the reasons I had hoped TechStars would be a great fit for Boston had come true, and then some.

Hundreds of investors jammed Microsoft's facility in Cambridge, Mass. to see the first TechStars investor day for the Boston program, held there in September 2009.

How TechStars Came to Seattle

Andy Sack

Andy is the managing director of Tech-Stars in Seattle, the co-founder of Founders Co-op, and the co-founder of Revenue Loan.

Photo by Randy Stewart

Anumber of people have asked me the story behind TechStars coming to Seattle. I first contacted David Cohen in January 2008. At the time, I had just started working on Founders Co-op and wanted to speak with David about his experience with TechStars. I thought that TechStars was on to something and I wanted to learn from what David was doing and consider doing something similar in Seattle.

Chris DeVore, my partner at Founder's Co-op and I decided we didn't want to mimic a three-month incubator in Seattle. In our opinion, TechStars was occupying that market space pretty well. I opted to start Founder's Co-op, a mentor-driven seed fund. When I spoke to David on the phone, he was kind enough to share some legal documents with me. Shortly after that call, I became a mentor of TechStars Boulder.

In January 2009, I learned that TechStars was expanding to Boston. I e-mailed David Cohen and Brad Feld and said that if they

ever considered expanding to Seattle I would be interested in working with them. David and Brad both encouraged me to spend more
time in the summer at TechStars to get to know the program. They
said that they were interested in exploring the possibility of working
together.

In May 2009, I went to my twentieth college reunion at Brown
University in Providence, Rhode Island. While I was back east, I
stopped by at the Boston TechStars 2009 orientation. It turns out
that Shawn Broderick, an old friend of mine from the 1990s Boston
technology scene was the managing director there. Shawn asked me
to speak to the incoming class of TechStars companies. I did—and
I'm not sure exactly what I said—but as I spoke I choked with emotion. The weekend had already been a trip down memory lane for
me—walking the campus at Brown already predisposed me to feeling
nostalgic. But I wasn't prepared for the raw energy emanating from
the founders of the Boston TechStars companies.

I spoke to the founders of those companies. I told them what
it was like for me to start Abuzz in 1996. I shed a few tears. I got
into my car and called Brad Feld and Jerry Colonna, the venture
capitalists who invested and bet on me and in Abuzz Technologies,
my first company. I decided then that Seattle needed a program like
this and that I wanted to run TechStars Seattle. Now, I just needed
David Cohen to be willing to open TechStars in Seattle.

In the summer of 2009, I made another two trips to Boulder in
an effort to get to know the TechStars program and David Cohen
better. After the second trip, David said that he was very interested in
opening TechStars Seattle but didn't want to make a decision until
October 2009. He also wanted to get to know the early stage technology scene in Seattle better. He went about meeting entrepreneurs
and investors in Seattle and even came to a Founder's Co-op LP
meeting.

By September 2009, David told me that he had pretty much
decided to expand to Seattle but he wanted the community of entrepreneurs to drive the expansion of the program. In early November 2009, there were a series of dinners in Seattle between Matt
McIlwain, Greg Gottesman, Brad Feld, David Cohen, and myself.

The next thing I knew, in a 24-hour period, Greg Gottesman
and David Cohen both called and asked me if I'd be willing to run
TechStars in Seattle alongside Founder's Co-op. After talking to my
partner, Chris DeVore, I enthusiastically agreed.

With the help of Greg Gottesman, I then approached the entrepreneur and venture capital community in Seattle and asked them to collaborate with us in supporting the launch of TechStars Seattle in August 2010. What happened was amazing! We received huge support from an incredible list of experienced entrepreneurs willing to act as mentors. In addition, nearly all the venture capitalists in the city elected to materially support TechStars in Seattle!

The list of investors includes:

- Jeff Bezos Investment Group
- Divergent Venture Partners
- Draper Associates
- Founders Co-op
- Foundry Group
- Ignition Partners
- Linden Rhoads (University of Washington Center for Technology Commercialization)
- Madrona Venture Fund
- Maveron Venture Capital
- Montlake Capital
- OVP
- Rolling Bay Ventures (Geoff Entress)
- Second Ave Partners
- Trilogy Equity Partners
- Voyager Capital
- Vulcan Capital (Paul Allen's group)
- WRF Capital

The Seattle startup scene has totally embraced TechStars and I think that the Seattle entrepreneur community is the big winner.

So You Want to Start TechStars in Your City?

David Cohen

David is a co-founder and the CEO of TechStars.

When I wrote this in early 2010, TechStars had been approached by serious representatives of more than 50 U.S. entrepreneurial communities that wanted to bring TechStars (or something modeled on it) to their city. This has been amazingly flattering and we've tried to help these folks however we can.

Part of helping has been having an open source philosophy about TechStars. We've published our complete results (see techstars.org/results), our seed financing documents (see techstars.org/docs), and have blogged and been interviewed extensively about our philosophy and approach to TechStars.

Earlier in this book, you read about our belief that quality trumps quantity. We could have built a franchise model and pumped out dozens of programs all over the United States. However, our belief was that we could not do this and maintain the same level of quality that we have had historically. We believe that others will replicate our mentorship-driven approach, and that this is generally a very good thing for entrepreneurship in the United States. That's why we're happy to be helpful, especially when we believe these efforts are credible.

I've said in several public interviews that I'll run TechStars forever as long as it doesn't lose money. Nothing is more gratifying. But rest assured, you don't create a program like TechStars to make money. You do it because you want your entrepreneurial community to be better. You do it because you understand that mentorship is the scarce resource for first-time entrepreneurs. You do it because you know that a culture of sustained mentorship will have a tremendous impact. You do it because you love your community, and because you love entrepreneurship.

We're not going to be dotting the country with TechStars programs. But if you're doing it for the right reasons and you're bringing meaningful, structured mentorship to bear, please know that we're your Number One fan.

I've been referring here to the United States. What about the rest of the world? I think that the TechStars mentorship-driven model can have an enormous impact around the world as well. We're already seeing similar programs throughout Europe. I've done some consulting on the model in places like Canada, Denmark, England, Japan, and Singapore. They're each remarkably different environments with their own drawbacks and advantages.

To all who have asked, for now, I can only say that this is about to become more interesting.

Appendix: The TechStars Companies

AccelGolf (2009)—offers mobile and online apps to golfers that improve their game through personalized content.—accelgolf.com

ADstruc (2010)—is an online buying platform for outdoor advertising that enables an auction and listing-based marketplace and makes the process of buying and selling faster and more profitable.—adstruc.com

AmpIdea (2009)—is helping new parents by offering services through a web-enabled baby monitor.—ampidea.com

AppX (2008)—provides software as a service to parties that invest in venture capital and private equity.—app-x.com

Appswell (2010)—is a mobile crowd-sourcing platform that allows people, companies, and brands to harness the wisdom of their crowds.—appswell.com

Baydin (2009)—creates e-mail utilities and collaboration catalysts that make e-mail even more valuable.—baydin.com

BlipSnips (2010)—makes it easy for users anywhere on the web to tag, share, and collaborate around memorable video moments.—blipsnips.com

Brightkite (2007)—lets you make friends, join communities, and share experiences on the go.—brightkite.com

BuyPlayWin (2008)—is the world's first tournament marketplace. Every shopper gets a chance—the chance to win their purchase by playing fun games against other shoppers.—buyplaywin.com

Daily Burn (2008)—is the premier fitness social network for detailed tracking, online accountability, and motivation.—dailyburn.com

Devver (2008)—takes the tools that developers use on their desktops and turns them into cloud-based services.—devver.net

Eventvue (2007)—helps conference organizers by providing an online community for the event and driving new conference registrations.—eventvue.com

Everlater (2009)—makes it simple to document, share, and remember travel experiences.—everlater.com

Filtrbox (2007)—is a new web service that tracks and monitors new media content and news for small-to-medium businesses as well as individuals.—filtrbox.com

Foodzie (2008)—is an online marketplace where consumers can discover and buy food directly from small artisan producers.—foodzie.com

GearBox (2010)—works with consumer electronics companies and developers to bring phone-controlled open devices to market.—gearbox.me

Graphic.ly (2009)—provides an immersive social experience and marketplace for digital comics and associated merchandise.—graphic.ly

Have My Shift (2009)—is an online marketplace for hourly workers to trade their shifts, allowing them to create the best work schedule.—havemyshift.com

Ignighter (2008)—is an online dating site with a unique twist—group-to-group dating.—ignighter.com

Intense Debate (2007)—replaces your standard blog comment system with a completely new tool for conversation.—intensedebate.com

J-Squared (2007)—is focused on social communication platforms and emerging technologies. Their applications are installed popular social networking systems.—j-squaredmedia.com

Kapost (2010)—lets anyone post to your site or blog, and you then control and filter those contributions. Develop a community of contributors to produce more and better content.—kapost.com

LangoLAB (2009)—is the most entertaining way to learn a foreign language.—langolab.com

Localytics (2009)—provides a real-time analytics platform for mobile applications.—localytics.com

LoudCaster (2010)—enables anyone to create an interactive online radio station.—loudcaster.com

MadKast (2007)—makes sharing blog posts simple and delivers detailed blog analytics to publishers.—madkast.com

Mailana (2009)—lets you share what really matters with the people who really matter.—mailana.com

Marginize (2010)—augments every page on the web with a space owned by the visitors where they can meet each other and interact freely.—marginize.com

Mogo (2010)—is a front-end testing and verification tool that helps companies ensure that their web sites render properly across various web browsers and platforms.—mogotest.com

Monkey Analytics (2010)—provides scalable data mining in the cloud.—monkeyanalytics.com

Next Big Sound (2009)—is online music analytics and insights.—nextbigsound.com

Occipital (2008)—is creating a human-computer interface which seamlessly augments the human sense of vision.—occipital.com

Omniar (2010)—is a better visual lookup for smartphones.—omniar.com

Oneforty (2009)—is the Twitter outfitter. It's the Twitter apps and services marketplace.—oneforty.com

People's Software Company (2008)—takes the pain out of making plans with your friends with planning and scheduling tools that plug in to your Facebook.—peoplessoftware.com

Rentmonitor (2010)—is a web-based property management tool for rental property owners. We take the paper out of the rental industry and to make it easy to be a landlord.—rentmonitor.com

Retel Technologies (2009)—develops video processing technology that provides online analytics for the offline world.—reteltechnologies.com

Rezora (2009)—is an e-mail marketing platform specifically designed for the real estate industry.—rezora.com

RoundPegg (2010)—is eHarmony for jobs. RoundPegg scientifically ensures personality and cultural fit for new hires.—roundpegg.com

ScriptPad (2010)—transforms the iPad and iPhone into a digital prescription pad allowing doctors to write prescriptions faster and safer than their current paper process.—scriptpad.net

Search-to-Phone (2007)—voice-enables the outdated Yellow Pages process by recording consumers' needs and then broadcasting that recording to local merchants.—searchtophone.com

SendGrid (2009)—is an e-mail service for companies sending application-generated transactional e-mail.—sendgrid.com

Sensobi (2009)—is personal relationship management for today's mobile professional.—sensobi.com

SnapABug (2009)—delivers faster customer care.—snapabug.com

Socialsci (2010)—is an online survey platform designed for scientific researchers.—socialsci.com

Socialthing! (2007)—is a digital life manager that puts what you do online into one place.—socialthing.com

SparkCloud (2009)—builds icebreaker tools and technologies to help us find people we should know.—sparkcloud.net

SpotInfluence (2010)—Spot Influence identifies influencers in social media from keywords.—spotinfluence.com

Spry (2009)—is detailed insight into software projects.—spryplanner.com

StarStreet (2010)—is the online sports stock market, where fans can leverage their knowledge of sports to make real money.—starstreetsports.com

StatsMix (2010)—allows companies to easily build and share custom dashboards for displaying and analyzing all the stats they generate.—statsmix.com

Tempmine (2009)—is an online temporary staffing marketplace—tempmine.com

The Highway Girl (2008)—is a show that educates artists on how to manage their careers in the digital age.—thehighwaygirl.com

Travelfli (2008)—Now UsingMiles, helps frequent flyers maximize the full potential of their loyalty programs.—usingmiles.com

TutuorialTab (2010)—lets companies make their web site more learnable.—tutorialtab.com

Usermojo (2010)—is an emotion analytics platform that tells you why users do what they do.—usermojo.com

Vanilla (2009)—is open source forum software.—vanillaforums .com

Villij (2007)—is a recommendation engine for people.—villij.com

Vacation Rental Partner (2010)—makes it easy to generate revenue from a second home. We offer tools that eliminate the need for traditional property management companies.—vacationrentalpartner.com

TechStars companies funded after publication are listed on the TechStars web site.

About the Authors

Brad Feld is a co-founder and managing director at Foundry Group, an early stage venture capital firm, and a co-founder of TechStars. Prior to Foundry Group, Brad co-founded Mobius Venture Capital as well as Intensity Ventures, a company that helped launch and operate software companies and later became a venture affiliate of the predecessor to Mobius Venture Capital.

Brad currently serves on the board of directors of BigDoor Media, Gist, Gnip, Oblong, Standing Cloud, and Zynga for Foundry Group. Previously, Brad served as chief technology officer of AmeriData Technologies. AmeriData acquired Feld Technologies, a firm he founded in 1987 that specialized in custom software applications.

In addition to his investing efforts, Brad has been active with several non-profit organizations and currently is chairman of the National Center for Women & Information Technology. Brad is a nationally recognized speaker on the topics of venture capital investing and entrepreneurship and writes widely read and well respected blogs at www.feld.com and www.askthevc.com.

Notable companies that Brad has invested in and/or sat on the boards of include Abuzz (acq. NYT), Anyday.com (acq. PALM), Critical Path (CPTH), Cyanea (acq. IBM), Dante Group (acq. WEBM), DataPower (acq. IBM), FeedBurner (acq. GOOG), Feld Group (acq. EDS), Harmonix (acq. VIA), NetGenesis (IPO), ServiceMagic (acq. IACI), and ServiceMetrics (acq. EXDS).

Brad holds Bachelor of Science and Master of Science degrees in Management Science from the Massachusetts Institute of Technology. Brad is also an avid art collector and long-distance runner. He has completed 15 marathons as part of his mission to run a marathon in each of the 50 states.

David G. Cohen is a co-founder and CEO of TechStars and is an investor in nearly 100 Internet startups.

Prior to founding TechStars, David was the founder and CTO of Pinpoint Technologies, which was acquired by ZOLL Medical Corporation (NASDAQ: ZOLL) in 1999. You can read about it in *No Vision, All Drive* (David Brown, Authorhouse, 2005). David was also the founder and CEO of earFeeder.com, a music service that was sold to SonicSwap.com in 2006. He also had what he likes to think of as a "graceful failure" in between.

Notable companies that David has invested in and/or sat on the boards of include Brightkite (acquired by Limbo), DailyBurn (acquired by IAC/InteractiveCorp), Filtrbox (acquired by Jive Software), Intense Debate (acquired by Automattic/Wordpress), Oblong, Plancast, SendGrid, SimpleGeo, Socialthing (acquired by AOL), StockTwits, and Twilio.

David is an active startup advocate, advisor, board member, and technology advisor who comments on these topics on his blog at DavidGCohen.com. He is also very active at the University of Colorado, serving as a member of the Board of Advisors of the Computer Science Department and Silicon Flatirons. David is also a member of the selection committee for Venture Capital in the Rockies, and runs the Colorado chapter of the Open Angel Forum.

David is recognized globally as a speaker on the topics of angel investing, Internet startups, and building local entrepreneurial ecosystems.

Acknowledgments

Our heartfelt thanks to Amy Batchelor, Jil Cohen, and all of the spouses, family, and significant others who put up with the entrepreneurs in their lives.

Our thanks also go out to Ben Casnocha, a TechStars mentor since 2007 and the author of *My Startup Life: What a (Very) Young CEO Learned on His Journey Through Silicon Valley*. Ben made many wise suggestions about the book that we quickly heeded. And he did it from Chile, around the time of the major earthquake there in early 2010. We are grateful that he is safe.

Our friends and amazing TechStars mentors Michael Zeisser and Paul Berberian both offered significant feedback about the structure of the book that we have incorporated here. We think their input has made the book approachable and interesting, which is something that they both are as well.

We are also grateful to Amy Batchelor, David's mother, Ginger Cohen, and Brad's mother Cecelia Feld for being such sticklers about the English language.

We also want to express our appreciation to David Brown and Congressman Jared Polis for co-founding TechStars with us and for helping to shape what it has become.

We appreciate the tremendous support from Brad's partners at the Foundry Group: Jason Mendelson, Seth Levine, and Ryan McIntyre, as well as Brad's assistant Kelly Collins.

Thanks are also due to past TechStars interns Al Doan, Gregg Alpert, and Cory Levy, who read early drafts of the book and offered candid and useful feedback.

We are very appreciative of the time taken and the insights provided by Phil Weiser.

Thank you to Andrew Hyde for his efforts with the TechStars community, and for many of the photos that appear in this book.

Thank you to multi-year TechStars gold sponsors Cooley Godward Kronish, Kendall Koenig and Oelsner (KKO), Slice of Lime, Holme Roberts and Owen (HRO), Metzger Associates, Square 1 Bank, Microsoft BizSpark, and Rackspace Cloud.

We cannot say enough about each and every one of the 150 TechStars mentors who donate their time and energy to help so many entrepreneurs. It is so gratifying to see what we have done together to have such a tremendous impact on our communities.

Finally, thanks to all of the TechStars mentors and entrepreneurs who contributed to this book. You are the greatest!

Index